# ADVANCED PRAISE FO

George Abraham writes, "i am always translati..g _____ ___ _ elements of Palestinian/universal displacement, immigration struggles, gender identity, body & memory as "fragmented countries" too, he has built a bold, brilliant book. His poems burn with questioning, "I was not always crumbled fortress & concrete/partition," they leap with energy. Here is a love too wide for containment, illuminating layers of story—family & land, political yet passionately personal. In a lineage of many broken hearts & heart attacks, here is a heart too brave to mutter or flail.

—NAOMI SHIHAB NYE, Young People's Poet Laureate

George Abraham is a "scripter of breath" who moves fluidly across poetic forms and linguistic borders to mourn the plight of the Palestinian people and to praise their resilience. Listen to these songs of exile, diaspora, and longing. Navigate these maps of home, the body, and belonging. Remember these translations of erasure, history, and inheritance. *Birthright* is a miraculous debut that "rewrites graves into sunrise" and crafts a poetics in which "every pronoun is a Free Palestine."

—DR. CRAIG SANTOS PEREZ, Author of Habitat Threshold

In George Abraham's poems, we discover the poetry of poetry, and in his hauntingly beautiful words, we discover the power of language. Abraham captures how politics penetrates our psyche and consciousness. He reflects on the loss of breath that results from Palestinian pain, but as his poems triumph through anguish, we are able to hold onto life. The journey of reading these words is also a universal one, bringing together conceptions of faith, love, family, settler-colonialism, violence, queerness, the search for home, and life and death. The aesthetic presentation, creativity, and raw passion of these poems is breathtaking, like nothing I have ever seen before. Never has poetry pierced through my heart, and touched my soul, as while reading Birthright for the first time. Abraham demonstrates that vulnerability is the ultimate form of strength.

—DR. SA'ED ATSHAN, Professor of Peace and Conflict Studies and Author of Queer Palestine and the Empire of Critique

We begin: "let me be brief: by the end of this someone will be cursed"—sit up straight. Take this book, lay it flat: the spine will crack, paper will flutter and then become waves to carry you over pages of answers to the overwhelming question at the center of your chest. A horizon waits, unfolding into the world ahead of you. Walk into it. Never stop—Birthright will have changed you. The forms this book moves through are striking: serving the speaker of the poems in all their attempts to experiment, to confront, to map, to unearth, to archive, and to build a home for a contentious identity. Abraham writes, "wandering, itself, can become a type of home"—each poem becomes a record of wandering, of the wondering. Each attempt a success of consistency that keeps opening into the unexpected. Each poem demands its own register of urgency. "Another entirely new species will emerge over generations," and is this collection not a new species of poetry? with prose broken & interwoven throughout, with the words weaving into kuffiyeh, with a literal Essay in the middle of the text, the binding energy throughout. An adrenaline like the reader is hiking along with Abraham a terrain both psychic and mythic before we reach the heart of it all: Palestine. The only thing Abraham is certain about. Birthright is prophetic, meta-aware, and necessarily dense. An essential honesty, a new kind of scripture. "how can anyone afford / forgiveness in a time like this?" Both sides of the epic tapestry of everything Abraham had to live to gift us this.

—**COMMUNAL STATEMENT** from Radius of Arab American Writer fellows (Jess Rizkallah, Summer Farah, Noor Hindi, Hazem Fahmy, and Noor Al-Ahmadi)

# BIRTHRIGHT

*poems*

George Abraham

—

Published by Button Poetry / Exploding Pinecone Press

Minneapolis, MN 55403 | http://www.buttonpoetry.com

—

Cover design: Amer Shomali

ISBN - 978-1-943735-67-9

23 22 21          2 3 4 5

*This book is dedicated to the Palestinian diaspora:*
*to the Land and the millions of people Birthed by it.*

# TABLE OF CONTENTS

# FOREWORD

In one of my recent workshops, a high school student of Saudi Arabian and Dominican heritage shared how he spent the majority of his early childhood convinced by his classmates, based solely on his physical appearance, that he was actually Indian. His richly complex heritage was reduced to fit the limitations of the [ongoing or residual] inherited colonial imagination. His imagined identity not-so-neatly repackaged to satiate that boundless learned human appetite to label and categorize; a failed and tiring ongoing taxonomy for a species that has yet to comprehend that we share 99.9% of the same DNA. Likewise, author George Abraham was a child in the second grade when he heard the word "Palestine" for the first time. "I was assigned a homework project investigating our family history. When my mother first said it, I went upstairs to my toy globe and could not find it anywhere." ("Ekphrasis on a Fragmented Nationalism")

If there were any doubt of the strength of the [colonial] imagination, I wouldn't have to point any further than these two examples and how they result in what can be described as an autoethnographic dysmorphia. Even in writing this, I reach for new terms that have yet to describe the experience of overturning the word "birthright." To examine its etymology. To free it of its connotations. To acknowledge that it exists because a people were denied it.

Within these pages, we examine the inverse of birthright. How do I write this without mentioning the obvious oppressor? An oppressor who deserves no more space in our minds, in our imaginations. I will their erasure in the writing of this and in the reading of Abraham's words. The violent existence of Israel, our complicity in allowing it. The ongoing genocide of Palestinian people and the rapid theft of their land and lives.

Through ingenious and formal experimentation, Abraham's *Birthright* points to this unending erasure by reclaiming, excavating and *un*-erasing. His is a dynamic lyricism that sings: Every nation, a failure. Every naming, an absence. Through a fine balance of inheritance and dispossession this work explores what it means to exist in simultaneity with grief and love.

Abraham teaches us how to read with a capital R. "I don't expect white people to understand how to Read this. I want them only to understand who I wish harm in the reading of me. Most of my family will die before reading this, and I think I'm okay with that." ("The Ghosts of the Exhibit Are Screaming [Palinode]")

These poems are comprised of form upon form upon form: Cento meets keffiyeh and Arabic meets Golden Shovel ("Ode to Mennel Ibtissam singing

Hallelujah on The Voice [France], Translated in Arabic") to make some of the most astonishing poetic forms you could imagine, making for a truly intersectional poetics in both content and form. His works are a restoration of country, history, body, identity, spirit and self. Every poem can be read as a point on a map. A non-linear and multi-dimensional map; a lineage; a cycle of trauma to be experienced and transmuted.

And in an act of incredible generosity, we journey with Abraham as he returns to his ancestral Palestine on his own birthright trip. "Even though we were in it, physically touching and breathing it, the city we were experiencing was the physical manifestation of the colonial imagination. I'm saying the blood was not only on our hands; the blood was in our minds. We were staring right into the heart of the beast . . . Our colonization doesn't just take the form of checkpoints, walls, eradicated villages, testimonies from families with concrete barriers through their houses; it is also opulence built over the wreckage, and residents who are convinced they live in the greatest city in the world. It was here, at this moment, I first realized my memory of Palestine was a misappropriation of my displaced family's experience, and no matter how much (un)learning I did, nothing would restore that original memory. Nothing would reconcile my experience of Palestine with my family's collective memory. Nothing would resurrect the country this once was."

Abraham is a visionary. "The liberated Palestine will not look like the Palestine that existed before it needed liberation. We must imagine it outside of its colonial reality." ("Ekphrasis on a Fragmented Nationalism")

I am grateful to hold this collection. A collection originally envisioned as a punchline arriving with Abraham's characteristic infectious laughter over tea and hookah in a New York City lounge.

This work speaks not only to the birthright of return but the right to our very own imaginations. An imagination that is free of colonial constructs, or is aware, at least, of those constructs' existence and the need to dismantle them—breath by breath, image by image, word by word, poem by poem.

M.H. HELAL

# BIRTHRIGHT

# TAKING BACK JERUSALEM

> "I said: you killed me . . . And I forgot, like you, to die."
> —Mahmoud Darwish

Let me be
        brief: by the end of this,
someone will be cursed & I pray it anyone

but Him. Let me start
        again: the night was beautiful but not
romantic. Sure,

there was smoke & moon
        -light. From this angle,
you could almost mistake the city

for *american*. There were 7, all of us born
        of this country before *this* country
existed. It was ours

the way a street cat is mothered
        by thin air. Still, we called this
a reclamation. A taking

back: the sign reading *cameras in use*
        outside an unlit jewelry store,
the palm trees dancing

like they could belong here—city of gravel
        throat & temple's cry—of gold
-blessed forehead & confluenced

histories—how many waters
        anointed & claimed you
inheritance? How many hands

un-sanctuaried you by birth
        -right & con
-quest? A name, however holy,

can be a story of unimaginable
        distance. We could only exit you
by the mouth through which we entered

& there, we first saw Him:
            shadow folded in shadow
speaking hushed & hurried Arabic,

& for the first time that night,
            a familiar I could but couldn't
have known: a Boy with moonlit tongue

promising His mother He'll make it
            back with every breath—peering
around the corner: a soldier, his

gun, that precise small
            -ness—I couldn't unsee him
or Him, couldn't uncast that smile

from his nodding face, our mouths
            pretty with english—he stopped
one of us. & searched

only one of us. & there, I remembered
            my mother, begging God to watch
over us in Jerusalem, where,

at 4 years old, a soldier held a gun
            to her head, & maybe it was or wasn't
at this exact spot, & maybe she prayed

for the wrong son, but in that moment
            I prayed. & there was no God
but the space between us—how the distance

between my holy & His
            holy could resurrect a broken
lord on my breath—& there I began

to understand how my mother could
            abandon her birthright—
& I suppose, she made it out.

Alive, depending on your frame
            of reference. & so did we. & by
some magic, so did that Boy, caught

with the wrong God on His
          breath in his holy city. Forgive me.
I'm trying to understand what makes

one's existence, at a fixed location, a radical
          act—divine even—& what makes
the existence of another, near a specific body

of water, a violence. Forgive me. I wrote this
          in an american airport,
& its magic escaped me.

# I. Dispossession

"Build me a city and call it Jerusalem. Build me another and call it Jerusalem. We have come back from Jerusalem where we found not what we sought, so do it over, give me another version, a different room, another hallway, the kitchen painted over and over, another bowl of soup."
—Richard Siken

# Inheritance: a Translation

I. *Song of Ash (Haifa, 2016)*

Filasteen is burning. It is
an obvious metaphor: for God
so loved the colonized, He sent us
to hell with our oppressors—for God
so loved us smoldering, He birthed us
unto ember topography, holy—leaking
light—hardly a metaphor at all.

\*

we were      first settler    intruder
who dared dance    on holy    land
as if it could ever be        ours—
then, we were      terrorist of
jealous      stone & flaming    tar
& now they paint        us arsonist
on our own      land & we're      exile
combustion        flying        rage
& isn't        that headline      worthy?
we're trending    & worth    attention
only in      anger—where      were your tears
& hashtags      when the fire      spread
to the West Bank?   when Gaza combusted
again?   & in August?   & in 2014?   & in 2008?

> *?reverse in read to hardest history isn't*
> *?repetition in digest to hardest it isn't*
> *?human when digest to hardest cremation isn't*

## II. *TEXTBOOK FRAGMENTS*

[ DNA TEST: IF YOU DRAW BLOOD / FROM A PALESTINIAN, BOIL / ITS SUBSTANCE UNTIL / IT BECOMES A TREMBLING[1] / SUBSTANCE, OF UNZIPPING / HELIX & DANCING VINE / PRACTICALLY AN ERASURE / OF ITSELF, THERE IS A ONE-IN-THREE CHANCE / THIS BODY SHARES / A CHROMOSOME WITH THE OPPRESSOR.[2] ]

[ CONSIDER IT *SOLIDARITY.* CONSIDER *DEFENSE MECHANISM* ]

[ NOTE: DO NOT CALL THIS WAR / GENOCIDE BUT INSTEAD, ETHNIC CLEANSING / PALESTINIANS NEED NOT LOOK AT / THE RACIALIZATION / OF IT ALL. THIS ENCOURAGES THE OPPRESSOR'S / POWER COMPLEX. MOST PEOPLE / IN THE MIDDLE EAST ARE WHITE / ANYWAYS[3] WHAT IS NARRATIVE IF NOT THE BLOOD / IT CARRIES? WHAT ARE YOU IF NOT THE TRAUMA YOU INHERIT?[4] ]

[ ~~ISN'T THIS BIOLOGY THE MOST OPPRESSIVE THING YOUR MOTHER GIFTED YOU~~ ]

---

[1] Whereas, the oppressor implants their DESIGN into every h(a)unted lineage—this country: everyone's inheritance.

[2] By which you mean, the oppressor runs through the bodies their bullets miss?

[3] By virtue of expulsion or white phosphorus?

[4] Every time i open my mouth: a chorus of BLOOD. i think of it as history.

the oppressor calls it
DIVERSITY or NARRATIVE
hence FABLE.

III. *Family History, in Reverse*

israeli man asks me to tie him up and fuck him. says he has a POWER COMPLEX.

after taking a sex hiatus, i contract mono. why does my BIOLOGY fail me?

(~~the first time i was raped i was outside myself~~)

the first panic attack in college feels like a heart attack. ER tech says i need sleep.

my parents fear college is making an *activist* of me:
>    *what happened to our son? why don't you come home anymore?*

*i eat hummus too, we're practically the same:* SOLIDARITY.

3rd grade: *you're dirty because you're Ay-rab.*
same year: baba almost dies of a heart attack.

age 6: i ask mama why we never visit palestine. why we never come home anymore.

my parents decide not to teach me arabic growing up: DEFENSE MECHANISM. or maybe i was never *theirs.*

teta dies of cancer before i'm old enough to understand. grape leaves blossom in her garden, little hands reaching for an invisible heaven like her BIOLOGY escaped her.

baba takes over shop at age 20 after sido dies of a heart attack. his mother, widowed in a country where no one speaks her language.

sido is forced out of Jerusalem at age 20. hence, mama is born in america. hence i am *american.*

settlement camps surround Ramallah, make an eviction notice of teta's house: cell MIGRATION. fatal OVERGROWTH.

the settlers took, first, the hilltops & aquifers. uprooted the olive trees & waged BIOLOGICAL WARFARE against us: reclamation. of INHERITANCE. (~~or was it GENOCIDE?~~)

when the colonizers emptied the villages, they lined up men to be executed in front of their families, raped women & planted pine trees over the wreckage. they were miles away from my teta's town. just far enough so no one could hear the screams:
*even when the land was ours,      it wasn't—*
(~~this is how i feel about my body sometimes~~)

## IV. *Binary.*

once i was a body & i was [male/female]. some days i contoured & dressed my [male/female] self & others i was spat out like a pit or seed uprooted from a digestible flesh. in either case i was [consumable/indigestible]. something to swallow & fill the void of every [rapist/lover]. how i turned [solid/fluid] in the presence of bone-shattering shear & chaotic tensors. how i puddled in my own redaction & swelled, stubborn, much like the blood who cannot unknow the turbulence it was born into. sometimes i feared my own [male/female] reflection, bestial like only a [terrorist/freedom-fighter] can know. the wrong historian refuses to call me [occupier/occupied]—says the truth lies [somewhere/ in-between], but i can think of no [conflict/ occupation] more clear than my own & isn't that worth a decisive history? no, i am not a refugee caught between the ash of two genocides. i cannot be in exile from somewhere i was [never/always] home in. i only know how to love in [fragments/categories]. so call me runaway ghost train. say i'm the mirror speaking back in shattered tongues. i am all of the question marks in your medical books. a [doctor/anthropologist] once tried to encode me into a binary rivulet—a sequence of 0's and 1's to name this digitized fluidity. but even in its purest form, i was still a mistranslation of [my/self].

V. *Lexicon of*

once, a language failed me & i hadn't a home
        to claim in my own throat—

in Arabic, the word for tonsil translates to *daughters*
        *of the ears*—we are taught

that to have a body is to carry
        its lineage inside of us—

& i've tried to make a language where my blood
        was just mine—but my tongue

rejected it. spat it out like a mouthful
        of Arabic—maybe it was defense

mechanism; maybe this is how i cough up blood—
        [ translation: how i cough up History ]

                        *


i once found home in the empty between clenched jawlines.
& that was the street my mother grew up—where *sand n*      came from
the mouth of a stranger, who was settler in this country.
        [ translation: what does an immigrant call it
                when they have no home to go back to? ]

                        *

i was never taught Arabic growing up
        [ translation—my father never wanted my *throat* to become *threat* ]
i don't watch the news any more
        [ translation—i am worried my people might be on it. ]
it is, as they say, tomorrow's history
        [ translation—hence always written by the victors ]
i mean to say, it repeats itself
        [ translation—i expect the obvious outcome; a *learned helplessness* ]
i saw a girl die on facebook & the video autoplayed
        [ translation—how do we mourn
                without a language to name our dead ]
the video repeated. & repeated. & repeated. &
        [ translation—i am always translating ]

VI. *Autotranslations of* Surveillance:

To call the florida suburbs our first lesson in loneliness: the only house on the
street to hang a flag that betrayed us because everyone hangs that flag here.
To hang the colonizer's god around our necks to call *salvation*. To call it *survival*.
To assemble, from every charred scripture, a word to call *God*.
To partition the mountains of a land to call *holy*, to build them into sniper towers.
To birth a police state & divinity in the same breath.
To inherit drought in unfamiliar currency, say *water is always holy once the wells dry*.
To become both floodwater & ebb; every iris, an ocean we refused to drown in.
To follow me on twitter, say *i reaaaaaaally like your poems*. To watchlist.
To track facebook videos of unarmed Palestinians being shot as *predictive policing*.
To pass unto everything your palm grazes, your oppressor's eyes. To midas touch.
To pray God watches over His people. To sing God watches over His people.
To love a land so much you could never trust that water.
To torture via water, starvation, sleeplessness, confinement to coffin-sized boxes.
To perceive every second faster than the one that preceded it: to approach death
in increasing velocities.
To carry the names of CIA torture victims in your family, yet everyone carries
those names here.
To respond *florida, usa* when the Tel Aviv checkpoint guard asks where you're
from. To be asked *are you sure,* despite.
To inherit a geography to call *american* & exist in the contradiction of it.
To write this poem, 2 oceans east, and be called *illegal*.
To un-name Dareen Tatour from this poem; to bleach Edward Said's name from
every tenure track.
To inherit a tongue of restless death & lexicon—a *rolling-in-our-graves* immortal.
To disappear, sobbing into a plate of falafel until it becomes *israeli*. To salt &
conquest.
To understand space only through finite temporal partitions: to claim any death as
*before our time* & exist in the cross-fire: it was death: it was a door: a light.
To exist, in the moment the bullet intersects the skin, at the border of three time-
frames simultaneously:

> *from the coordinate frame of a gun, every bullet is an exile spat out of its country; from
> the frame of a country, everyone is a gun to be bullet-filled; from the frame of the bullet,
> there is no home aside from the torrid air that lifts it—*

To exist, at once, as both object & verb in every tense—
To pass unto our children, this inherited paranoia, anxiety, its collapsing timescale,
hence making the police state timeless, hence God—
To laugh after being put on the watchlist, say *finally you fuckers*—to be a *laughing-in-
God's-face* type of immortal—
To lean into the light, as if it was jealous enough to take us back; as if we weren't
ancestored before even drawing our first breaths—

## VII. *Annihilation Landscape (Nakba)*

what the textbooks fail
to mention: i was whole
once. this flesh, not always
a reddened ecosystem; these rose
-soaked kuffiyat, not
a thousand ghosts' of
dancing—i was not

always crumbled citadel & concrete
partition. once, the bodies
in me could sing without
screaming—

how the trees whisper
a different nation's wind
-song; how roots grasp
buried kin like only a mother
could; even when life
is planted in me, they make
amnesia of my childrens'
laughter, call my hollow
false witness. the question marks
in your books—i am an erasure

of myself—my biology
fails me—once
i had a body
to choke on

## VIII. [ CONFLICT/OCCUPATION ]

i open my mouth & a severed tongue falls out. i call this [       ].
yesterday i swallowed a crystalline liquid, *a white witch's tears*, a friend
joked & i became a pantomime—how i am most at home when
outside

myself. today, a needle pierced the bridge of my nose, my skin
bubbled, retreated from the puncture the way one escapes a burning
country & that was [       ].

forgive me. i promised, this wouldn't be a poem about my body. or
Palestinian [       ] but it is always

both. i contour my face with sand & it is war paint. i puncture my
nostril with steel & that is war crime. a hamsa dangles from my
earlobe & the room empties itself

& here i am. is this what you mean by arab witchcraft? that you could
mistake this ~~skin~~ for anything but mine—& isn't that the perfect

[       ]? the Queerest [       ]? tell me you didn't mistake me for the
slowest lullaby & i'll say: i have so many bodies in me—if you look
close enough,

you could almost mistake me for a massacre.

IX. *Mistranslations of Ash (Haifa, 2016)*

When a country commits suicide, do we mourn
      first the land or the bodies ensnared
      by its brief promise of home? Yes,
            even cities get tired of waking.

     *

Sido said Haifa was ceaseless
sunset—light painting Mediterranean
anything but crimson, pouring through palm
trees like sand through naive fingers, unknowing
      of land's embrace—

     *

The first time i used the word *depression*
with my parents, they said *but you're so happy
here*—couldn't marvel the sight
of their radiant house in flames: *i fear
a horizon free of crimson,* i wanted
to say, *my mind is a country
that sets itself ablaze*

X. █████ *History*█████ [ WITH ZIONIST TRANSLATIONS ]

israeli man ~~asks me to tie him up and fuck him. says he has~~ [GIVES HIMSELF TO A PALESTINIAN WITH ] a POWER COMPLEX.

~~after taking a sex hiatus, i contract mono. why does my~~ ~~BIOLOGY~~ ~~fail me?~~
████████████████████████

~~the first panic attack in college feels like a heart attack. ER tech says i need sleep.~~
[ YOUR BIOLOGY IS IRRELEVANT IN THIS POLITIC. ]

my parents fear college is making an ACTIVIST of me.
        *what happened to our son?* [ WITNESS THE PARENTS RECOIL AT THE BEAST THEY SPAWNED. ] ███████████████████████████████

*i eat* [ISRAELI]*hummus too~~, we're practically the same~~: ~~SOLIDARITY.~~* [A PEACE OFFERING. ]

████ *you* █ *dirty* ████ *you* █ *Ay-rab.*
[ YOU SAID IT. WHY DO PALESTINIANS ALWAYS TEACH HATRED AMONG THEIR OWN? ]

█████████████████ never █ palestine. █████████████

my parents ████ teach me ████████████████
████████ ~~i was never~~ *~~theirs~~* teta dies ████████ old
enough to understand ██████████████
█████ invisible ████████████████

baba takes over. ████████████ sido ██████ a██████
██████ country where no one speaks

~~sido is forced out of Jerusalem at age 20. hence, mama is born in america. hence i am~~ *~~american.~~* [ WE WERE STATELESS ONCE; SUPPOSE HE WAS SETTLER IN *OUR* HOME.]

settlement camps ~~surround~~ [REVIVE] Ramallah~~, make an eviction notice of teta's house~~: cell MIGRATION. fatal OVERGROWTH. [ YOU ALWAYS KNEW US TO BE CANCEROUS. YOUR BLOOD LIBELS & TALK OF LIBERTY CLOG THIS LAND LIKE ARTERIES.]

~~the settlers took, first, the hilltops & aquifers. uprooted the olive trees & waged~~ ~~BIOLOGICAL WARFARE~~ ~~against our lineage~~: reclamation. of INHERITANCE.

[ & WHAT IF THE SETTLERS WERE FLEEING RELIGIOUS PERSECUTION, MUCH LIKE PILGRIM SETTLERS FLED FOR AMERICA. WAS IT *COLONIZATION* THEN? OR *PROMISE*? ] (~~or was it GENOCIDE?~~) [ BY VIRTUE OF EXISTING, YOU ARE A GENOCIDE. ]

~~when the colonizers emptied the villages, they lined up the men to be executed in front of their families, raped the women & planted pine trees over the wreckage. they were miles away from my teta's town. just far enough so no one could hear the screams:~~

██████ *the land* ████████ *wasn't.*

(~~this is how i feel about my body sometimes~~) [ YOU CAN'T SAY YOU WEREN'T ASKING FOR ANY OF THIS. ]

## XI. *Song of Ash (Ghazal)*

My people carry another sunrise on their backs;
bear the ashes of two diasporas on their backs;

Scapegoat of hellfire, stone shrapnel,
& false Gods on their backs;

Of riot shield blockade; of night doused
in teargas & steel jaws on their backs;

Moonlight, thick with arabic & white
phosphorous, shines full on their backs;

A thousand flags, white & heavy,
to eviscerate flesh off their backs;

To rebuild & smolder on; to build dusk
from dawn with a whole country on their backs;

To reteach living, unlearn the mouths
& white lies on their backs;

Haifa burns & cries wolf, cries Palestine,
cries repentance on their backs;

Gaza burns & burns again, & the silence
weighs heavy on their backs;

The fire consumes all: cyclical inheritance.
The fire weighs heavy on their backs—

## apology

it is the summer after my spleen almost ruptured into the stain of a thousand sunsets: i am sitting in a therapist's office: & she asks me to start at the moment i wanted to die from my own hands: i could have painted her my body: in all its failed topologies: i haven't a home that isn't in love with its floodwaters: but instead: i decide to say: 1967: the west bank is annexed by israel after nakba: my grandparents: exiled: when i say anxiety stretches continents: when i say depression is an ocean we never wanted to traverse: 1988: my aunt falls in love with a woman twice her age: finds mother in her after her own grieved a stolen country: decades of a husband with fists: for blood: when she comes out they ask if she needs to see a therapist: a nice woman to excise this demon in her: today: a stranger with fists makes a growing country of my organs: & calls it a topology lesson: a stranger who cannot recognize me tells the class of exact sequences: how topological spaces inherit the shape of their emptiness from previous generations of dimensions: a whole lineage of singularities & at this point i too want to disappear: in the office of this therapist: who is perhaps a topologist: who asks *so what shape does this anxiety take inside of you?* & i want to say: tooth of a mouth: eye of a hurricane in my chest: organ with vast chambers haunted by their own empty: & so much blood it can almost be mistaken for a country: newfound inheritance: faithlessness found at the intersection of 3 merciless gods: *do you pray still? why have you stopped praying?* the therapist asks: & perhaps the therapist is my mother: who found god at the bottom of crimson bottles: who prayed for a son that left: in search for Home: desire swelling in him like a ruptured organ: father forgive me: my drunk inheritance: forgive the stairs that collapsed beneath the weight of me: the third floor window that almost swallowed me into the night's mouth: forgive the bodies i swallowed: like broken teeth: the knees i spent trying to summon god in my own: forgive my DNA strands for they are sculptors of brief suicides: i'm trying to love the shattered window of myself: the hands: the rocks: the broken religion left behind: my inheritance: this body of vandalized cathedrals: light me on fire: strip my god from my breath: watch as i dance amidst the flames:

## Index, for the damned

the first time a boy craved
me, he said *i want what my god refuses*

*me*, his fingers gracing
my young lips; we were home

alone, & the blood wanted
what it could not conjure; i wanted

him, fist & rapture; i hadn't
a language where affirmation wasn't a self

-sabotage, so i let boyhood answer
his call, & my breath was not

my breath; my lips, captives
begging a collapsing

tomb of his, thick, & ungodly
the refuse which parts atria; he still called me

*fucking queer*, & i have since known *queer*
to mean *desire my god*

*rejected.* or
*forsaken.* blood of

lamb. think sacrilege, crucifixion
by mouth, much like *luti*, translated people

of Lot; sinners of Sodom; maybe if I meant
*no*, i wouldn't be sin

& exile in every language
that claims me; i want لا to lack desire's

tangibility, unlike نعم which, birthed heavy
in the lungs, can corrode

breath, hence *un*voice; in this language,
let us make every *no* as inescapable

22

as the voice it clings to; a gentle
Ɣ can kiss the tongue & close

a throat in the same breath, & i
wonder if that too is a self

-colonization; to un-mother the mouth,
strip the altar its sacrifice; let me be,

instead, a lighthouse; let me converge
at the point where all wanderers

intersect unwounded, even in
want; if desire is,

as my language translates, *a moon*,
let me be the satellite which learned its own

escape velocity; let my words, instead of endless
litany, be an index unhinging every name

forced upon us, & let that be biblical. watch us
rewrite graves into sunrise—ceaseless

fractal—call us scripters
of breath for every silence that failed

us; for every trachea collapsing
under its own weight—

# incomplete confessions of wind

The sand is coming. Listen: no whisper aside from the atlantic's
low hum. The absence illuminated in particle. Only there were boys

with sandpaper skin. The sand was white and so it was vast. The boys
needn't fear the ocean, nor did they fear their father's blue. They could

and couldn't have come from it, those minerals, dead and without
carcass—still, the boys held the shells like they would a strip

of bark, always a breakage before the hurl into an unknown
displacement. The moon was vast and so it was white, at this precise

distance. The boys didn't see it, off in the distance, the sand
falling mid-air in sheets. There was a towel six feet to my left, dancing mid

-flight like a ripped flag. Like instinct, i wrapped it around my face as if
i knew how to survive this landscape & the boys,

silenced to their core. When birthed by midnight
sandstorm, the boys held me in their mouths like they would

*Raghead*—    they didn't say it aloud. They needn't give it voice: the boys,
unmoving. White as bone, plucked & bleached for exhibit. In truth, my skin

betrayed them. The boys with strawmat hair—i think one
was named jake—how he too reached for shelter, asked if i could help him

become me, like i wasn't warned of hands ghosted into land's
negative. Like i didn't recognize that face, rancid & speechless

the way, when cut open, a gall-bladder can leave an entire room gasping
& nauseous.   The wind subsided. Perhaps i made it

all up—it was as if nothing happened: the boys resuming their small
-ness. A breeze receding into lullaby— there was nothing left to say—my feet

shifting between salt & mineral, sinking into that earth,
unsteady— as if i was digging my own grave—

## origin story, age 17, to be written on the walls of my childhood house in blood

so it's the night of my birthday: my 2 party guests & i went to a horror movie i've already seen bc the party guest i had a crush on hadn't seen it yet, but i didn't mind really bc it was scorpio season & i was a Spooky Bxtch™ who liked Spooky Bxtch™ movies & the movie was . . . gooood? the way white suburban afternoons were . . . *goood?* or predictable & full of jump scares & after the movie we got taco bell, despite national headlines' horsemeat rumors lol, & when we returned mom asked if we ate anything & we lied & she still brought out a plate of mah'shee, which my white friend found disturbing yet oddly charming, & that night, we cut the cake but did not eat it; the boy i found beautiful left early to see his blonde & unremarkable girlfriend &, as soon as all two of my guests were gone, i went back to my room as if i expected anything less of tonight than this: my parents falling asleep in different rooms; the boy i wanted falling asleep in different arms; the distance between my bed & his; the tree shedding its lonely moss outside my window—yes, that was the first night i considered committing suicide. & i could not say it was the first night i didn't love myself; i hadn't the language to diagnose this self-emptying, despite the psychology class that gave me words wrapped in sterile gauze & fluoxetine, despite my mother & the days she'd stumble out of the back door in search of a second bottle bc the first didn't put her to sleep in broad daylight & father, who says *therapy is for amarkan*, calls both of us ungrateful & blames me for the day mama crashed her minivan into a concrete pole after the sun caught her eye, or at least that's what she told the cop when she passed out at the wrong bend in the road & when the cop asked if we, her children, felt safe with her driving us back, i wanted to say, *i do not blame my mother for her dry drowning*; the nights she'd remind me i was stuck in hell with her bc she couldn't leave, nor could she imagine the wings i'd grow: yes, i inherited my mother's hands: i know how to disappear, silent as the repentance after the prophesized bloodshed; silent as, the first man i ever loved telling me he's dating a white woman; silent as, my father saying pansexuality is *something the internet made up*; silent as scraping my knees on the church's uneven pavement & seeing my bones for the first time; silent as another apology, my mother repenting to a god she loves even in drowning & aren't we all invisible-reaching? my parents once built me a sanctuary & it almost killed me. my mother found sanctuary in my father & it almost killed her. my grandparents once found sanctuary in america after the land they called sanctuary was stolen & that too almost killed all of us— my mother tells the story like this: as an infant, a bird once swooped down, stole my hotdog from its bun, & flew off. she says i broke down & sobbed. i can't remember it exactly, but i'd like to think that was the most honest history ever written abt any of us.

# Triptych with Varying Degrees of Certainty, Posed as an Interrupted Sestina

I.       incomplete confessions of earth
         or, *your father contemplates his family history while outside of himself*

       yes, those were your 3amo's hands
       knocking the tiny tongue of a gun
       chattering, in imprecise momentum,
       while you trembled behind a splintered door—
       your small-mouthed amygdala—sweating
       backfired diamonds: a familiar anatomy.

       your 3amo's liver, a languid anatomy,
       translated blood into language of hands,
       crooked & rapid fire; his palms sweat
       tiny oceans into chokehold, the gun
       stained of coin & ghost of brother, come door's
       buck & shear, come ramshackle momentum

       & neck twitch—your familiared momentum
       beneath bulb's flicker; your colorless anatomy
       illuminated in coin count—the shop's door
       also in translation—dead in your white hands,
       faces bulleted in metal. come glass & shatter & gun
       pressed to your temple's brief crater, sweat

       -lined, the bullet. fathered. his hands: yes: their sweat
       & shake of devil's tongue: his and: your momentum:
       wall-shocked: smoke of: your father's: gun:
       a punctuation mark: swelled into: intuder's anatomy:
       or was it your 3amo: leaking red: instead of his mother's hands
       in endless prayer, it was the shop's closed door

       that could not forget him: dead & white: door
       with a penny-splintered amygdala, whose sweat
       stained the air humid. your quivering hands

in restless autumn: you stared into a leaf's momentum
& could not unsee the bloodshed of your own anatomy:
in truth, you couldn't leave your poor mother by gun—

in truth, every man in your family was once a gun
cabinet: house of nickel bullet & mahogany door:
every footrail south, splayed with fibrous anatomies,
white on red: un-oceaned the musculature of its sweat:
a history, precise & calculated in its momentum,
remembered only in soil: the work of your own hands:

II.     Against Honesty: a catalogue of imperfect endings

Because I had too many words in my mouth but none
of them were enough, I leaned into their incantation
like a spell of godless repetition to witness

my father held at gunpoint by a white nationalist,
or my father held at gunpoint by his own 3amo,
or the memories not being mutually exclusive—

all of them colored in sweat & momentum, gun &
door, but in truth, my grandfather was the only one
who fired, & sure, I can call that *empire collapsing*

*into a single man*, or I can call *that immigrant collapsing*
*into empire's choke*, but I owe nothing to Truth, who
once considered our people nonexistent—tell me

you haven't lied to construct an honest history,
or that they were just brothers on the wrong end
of a bruise, or ghost story, or digestible myth—

My Teita would tell his story like this: when he was
a child with grass knotted between his fingernails,
sweating every color in that tiny & wondrous anatomy

beneath a forgiving sun, the back door would swing wide
open, humming with fruit flies, & that momentum meant
summer had already begun, the shovels were already staked

in the yards, & it was during that season, when he tended
the garden of his neighbor—a dying woman who, come nightfall,
gifted him a single fern which, when planted, would erupt

into an ocean of hands in his backyard, & said *let the land*
*remember every history we cannot inherit*; how they sprawled into
a multitude—that wind, an endless, swaying music.

I don't remember a time he ever laid a hand on me.

III.       complete confessions of earth
         or *you*      *contemplate*       *history*       *of*   *self*

yes: those hands: tiny guns: translated blood: into choke: anatomy
colorless: in translation: every man in your family was once:
un-oceaned: hands in endless prayer: the work of your own:

## Heritage

Come morning, he won't even remember my name.
Come midnight, we'll be washed of his every trace:

the blood pooling in moonlight, staining oceans
empty of biology's brief mimicry. I said *I love him*

because he too was born on the wrong side of a wall;
perhaps, in funeral quiet, this is the whitest he'll ever be.

We thank him for his service behind a makeshift altar—
& what of gratitude isn't a thinning bloodline?

His head pillowed by flag of blood & star. In life,
he'd cook for us. He never let us leave empty-stomached.

His brother grips my hand. Asks *what are you?*
Transfixes his eyes on the wounds I bulleted into my own face.

All he knows of divinity was once heresy & clipped wing.

In truth, had they known of the mouths I spoke a swollen
history into, most men in my family would have wanted me

dead, & I'd like to think this its own forgiveness—
into the gardener's hands, both seed & floodwater;
the expense of every bloom, a season of winded upheaval—

because who else would know better this swallow
& fang-sunk tongue? Because they've tasted their own

pooling blood, I'd like to think my ancestors couldn't imagine
me unwritten from their gospel—the ghosts that wear my name,

not the exiles of another heaven: inherited,
because we too lost our countries before we lost our bodies.

Every man I've held with pen was once capable of breaking me.
We were never meant to survive this mythos.

Forgive me. I'm running from this poem, into another boy's arms like

we were never meant to survive this mythos.
Every man I've held with palm was once capable of breaking me

because we lost our countries before we lost our bodies;
not the exiles of—another heaven inherited

me from unwritten gospel—the ghosts that wear my name
pooling blood; I'd like to think my ancestors couldn't imagine

this fang-sunk tongue because they've tasted their own;
because who else would know better this swallow—

the expense of every bloom, a season of winded upheaval
into the gardener's hands, both seed & floodwater;

& death, I'd like to think, is its own forgiveness—
its own history—most men like him would have wanted a family in me,

in truth, had they not known of the mouths I swelled into.
All we know of heresy was once divinity's un-clipped wing.

He transfixes his eyes on the wounds I bulleted into my own face.
He grips my hand, asks *what are you      wanting?*

He cooked for me, after. He'd never let me leave empty-stomached.
My head, pillowed by stars of no flag. In life,
what of gratitude isn't a thinning bloodline?

I thanked & serviced him behind our makeshift altar
in funeral quiet. Perhaps this is the whitest I'll ever be—

Although he too was born on the wrong side of a wall,
empty of biology's brief mimicry, I couldn't have said *I love you*:
our blood, pooling in moonlight, staining oceans—

come midnight, I'll wash myself of his every trace.
Come morning, I won't even remember his name.

# elegy for Home in mirrored graves, ending with a collapse of wings

I.        for D—

it is the winter after my aunt swelled into a human
bruise, & tonight is the last night i'll spend in this white suburban burial
mound. father hints at moving out, recalls the hauntings

this house gifted him:   footsteps echoing in      empty —furniture's
slight   perturbations, jewelry misplaced despite the saint anthony statue
we buried, like all the religions that failed us,   & now my father

does not go to church; our dead have begun speaking to him
in dreams: his father, who built this house after fleeing
dispossession, warns my father that this very land wants us dead,

& maybe that is not a metaphor: how my aunt was found
dead in a white trailer park that celebrates its heritage in massacre:
here, an israeli flag rippling synchronously with an american flag,

diametrically opposed to a confederate flag; hear the wind heavy
with howling & contradicting histories—the walls pinned with flesh
unrecognizable; when the police found my aunt, they declared her death

an *overdose*, despite her neck's handprint bruises; her inheritance being not this
blue-faced death, but the silence after; how florida swallowed her whole, & so
history repeated itself in another brown queer woman, & now,

by existing, this house is but another erasure of dispossession; another
unwriting: how this land once belonged to the Indigenous Timucuan,
until the settlers came with viruses, guns, eliminating the population tenfold

& calling it *territorial expansion*; i grew up miles away from the remnants
of an extinct, unwritten people & was taught to have pride in this
country; to wave the flag & not confront its legacy; call jacksonville a city

of *immigrants* & rewrite our dispossession into another—& isn't that how
this all began? hasn't this always been a ghost story? how white imperialism
scapegoated Jewish survival after genocide, ash, earth turned hell; hence israel

exists, hence, belonging nowhere, we exist among the restless dead
we trample over; maybe florida is an unmarked grave; america too, the largest
unmarked grave. can i call it home if there aren't corpses caught in its teeth?

if its roadways aren't endless arteries leading to no heart  at all?

31

II.       for Em—

if this were an honest elegy, i would say i loved her like i could only love
a sister i have & haven't died for. in truth, she was white & so she was family
enough to scare my father pale—the way he feared her reflection

before she swore every chandelier into a rattling phantom; maybe a ghost
is just a ghost—or my mother when refracted in crystalline; would you
believe me if i called her my last reason to return? & now, i cannot

drive back without another haunting: here's the street we made
an endless summer of: yellowcard singing, *this is how it feels to not be*
*-lieve*, like they too understood what it meant to fly & never look back

& always be looking back; once, we found home in sunset & walked into it,
hand in hand; once, her curls trapped the moonlight & that was the first time
i believed in god; once, i fled into an angel's arms before my escape

of wings & the story did not end there; the story did not end
in grace, like that of every country we built before it turned to blood
-shed; before we ever had ghosts to mourn: an asymmetrically torn

ticket stub, a secretly passed post-it note with i's dotted in hearts, coffee
stain obscuring the quantum physics, as if that too wasn't a memoryless
thing, sunglasses studded in fake diamonds collecting dust by now—

the ones she left in my car the night i came out to her in a walmart
parking lot; she, the first friend i came out to, hence family, & now
i am the last known queer person alive in my family, & my father has never

been so Christian, even though he "doesn't know"—perhaps he feared
because he thought i couldn't have loved her & so he turned skyward
in a lone symphony of asynchronous clocks; yes, i made a god

-fearing man of—    my father,      not even knowing      the days i wanted
     to unbecome           beneath the very roof      he built; he could not see
the writing       on the walls—     the lives i could end with      an open

window,      in metaphor      or not,      & though i did not       fly that night,
i fled:    my own winged        migration; yes, i flew north       for the winter
to avoid     Winter; yes,        my wings conjured    a constellation   of hurricanes

on the way;    the irony      being, i made     a dispossession    of myself;
yes, history     repeated       itself   in me; i built        shelter from dust

& bone, from mud      & twig, & that is     not to say i exorcised myself

of the demons      seeking to make       a stain of me, but it is   to say

i survived   them, am surviving      them, & doesn't     that make

me miracle?      how i fled      home without      dissolving into salt

pillar—            i mean, i        fled. i fled. i        flew

     & in spite of      my invisible            breakings

       again &                      again &

          again            &      again


                         i fly—

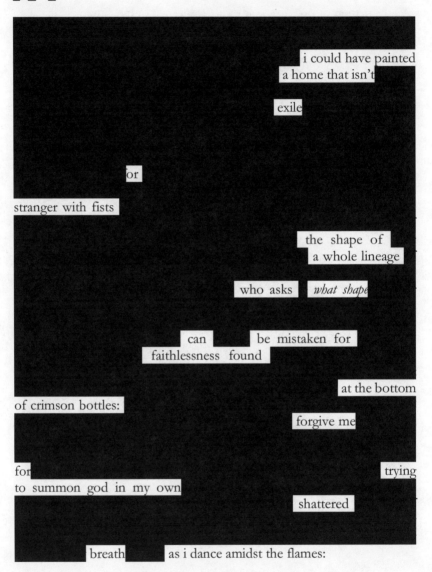

i could have painted
a home that isn't

exile

or

stranger with fists

the shape of
a whole lineage

who asks   *what shape*

can         be mistaken for
faithlessness   found

at the bottom
of crimson bottles:

forgive me

for                                                                trying
to summon god in my own

shattered

breath          as i dance amidst the flames:

# II. Birthright

"I am singing a song that can only be born after losing a country."
—Joy Harjo

## Video Loop : Ben Gurion Airport panic attack

*israel: land of creation*

     \*

Travel Advisory:
תיירים יכולים לוותר מתביעה לפי
דולר סחורה 200
tourists can forego claiming
under 200 USD in merchandise
يمكن للسياح التخلي مدعيا تحت
200 دولار أمريكي في البضائع

     \*

man points / camera in / -wards,
kisses / his wife, lips/ curling in sunset

     \*

woman in white
-face, opera house
vignette—strips skirt
flesh bare against
the spotlight's glare
seeking sunlight—

     \*

Travel Advisory:
    the following are prohibited:
    weapons/ عملاء كيميائيين /
    المواد الإباحية / الكحول
    أكثر من 3 أوقية من العطور

     \*

*israel: land*
*of creation*

     \*

violinist touches string as he might
a lover—soft vibratto, wrist
a delicate symphony—lips to
metal tube      zoom out // spotlight

[ a couple making aaliyah / cuts in front of / the teleprompter—
baby/ in hand, 3 children / in their shadow ]

        *


*it's been an hour // since they took Z // at security—he was // the only ~~dark-skinned~~ muslim
// in our group // my cross hangs heavy // around my throat // name // blood~~line~~*

        *


Travel Advisory:
        beware of *prohibited* materials
        beware of أسلحة
        tourists can forego (~~themselves~~)

        *


*israel:*
*land of*
*creation*

            *


[Tel Aviv shoreline]—sunset, a bearded man
kicks a soccer ball—a couple's curled lips
& countries—spoils of (*90 minutes // Z*
*isn't back*) knife, caressing wine glass
full of another blood          again—

        *


the couple is gone. the airport, empty
aside from our collective pulse—
i re-activate facebook
& relay the good news—
        *i'm Home*

                        (no word from Z )
        *i'm finally*        Home—

# in which you do not ask the state of israel to commit suicide

The officers, speaking harsh fragments, run your boots through the security scanner 3 times. You are given a red name badge to wear, but they keep your passport at the front desk. You are instructed not to ask questions.

Eventually, 2-by-2, in 5- to 15-minute intervals, the waiting room begins to fill with your American classmates, marked with blue badges and blue passports in their hands. A sign reading *Israeli Ministry of Foreign Affairs: security cameras in use* prompts your friend to joke about the room being bugged. She is also wearing a red badge. Her voice is the first thing to remind you of home.

Eventually, you are ushered into a large lecture hall. A dark-skinned woman stands at the podium. You see her last name flash across the screen and are relieved by the familiar space it occupies in your mouth. The woman introduces herself as an Iraqi Jew who was now a political law advisor to the israeli state. She begins explaining the difficult legal nuances of counter-terrorism, saying the terrorists place unfair pressure on israel to operate on a higher moral ground. She who had a terrorist name. She who speaks both terrorists' languages. She who grew up living among terrorists, now drops bombs on behalf of a state that builds her into their acceptable terrorist.

The speeches proceed & blur as the politicians recite rehearsed arguments, none of which are unfamiliar. Your haze breaks when the last speaker, a white-haired man, starts answering audience questions & says, "1948 happened. 1967 happened. And we won. This is war, I mean, things like this happen."

His stare, gray and rigid as stone. You lock eyes with a Palestinian woman, who responds: "so what you're saying is, my mother, who was born in Haifa, cannot return, but any random american Jew can?" That, too, was familiar to you.

"Listen," the man sighs and removes his glasses. "I don't know your mother, but I assume she can find a home in another Arab country. If we were to accommodate every refugee who claims this land, that would, in essence, be asking the state of israel to commit suicide. I hope this answers your question."

You want to say you're surprised by all of this, but in truth you're just numb. Or maybe the language has already escaped you.

An hour later, you are ushered out of the room by a woman who is introduced to you as an intern. You attempt to make small talk with her, only to receive half-smiles and nods. The security guard at the front desk hands back your passport, saying, "she doesn't understand your language."

# Broken Ghazal, Before Balfour

"It being clearly understood that nothing shall be done which may prejudice the civil
and religious rights of existing non-Jewish communities in Palestine."
—The Balfour Declaration, 1917

It being clearly understood that the gazelle was not
always a border between extinct and endangered.

It being clearly understood that ground sumac & the heart of a pomegranate
are proof enough that a country can coagulate in our hands.

It being clearly understood that every image of Elysium came from somewhere;
that inside every heaven there is an earth we've mourned the loss of.

It being clearly understood that wandering,
itself, can become a type of home.

It being clearly understood that *there was never a Palestinian people*, came from
the mouth of a settler who, when asked *where are you from*, replied *Chicago*.

It being clearly understood that the settler's father
was "Palestinian" by his own definition.

It being clearly understood that, in his childhood, Sido would wander
the streets of Jerusalem with his Jewish neighbors every morning.

It being clearly understood that
they fell out of touch.

It being clearly understood that, while the gazelle is the most Palestinian thing to
write about, I've never seen one. I'm starting to think we made them up.

It being a clearly understood
mythology.

It being clearly understood that
*Israel's Right To Exist.*

It being clearly understood that, when our cathedrals & mosques were
burning, there was never anything to mourn.

It being clearly understood that our churches were built before
        their ancestors' ancestors' ancestors knew Christianity existed.

It being clearly understood that *the church will use their best endeavors*
        *to facilitate the achievement of this object.*

It being clearly understood that this object,
        *which may prejudice the civil and religious rights of existing*
        *which may prejudice the civil and religious rights of existing in Palestine.*

It being clearly understood that
        Palestine.

It being clearly understood that *His Majesty's Government views with favor.*
        *The establishment in.*                              *Any other country.*

It being clearly
        religious.

It being clear.

Understood.

## in which you do not ask the state of israel to commit suicide

"What you have to understand about 1948 is they not only destroyed our village; they destroyed our lives." Yacoub's voice crackling through the bus mic's static almost resembles your grandfather's. The way he'd pause and let "ya'ani" bridge the countries in his sentences: "ya'ani, this was my home. My childhood. My paradise."

The bus shifts left to exit, Hebrew signs painting the side of the road, as you approach what remains of Lifta: mountainside speckled with stone remnants, structures half-standing, swallowed by the overgrowth.

Your moments in Lifta begin to blur: first, the descent, steep, as if the land itself is beckoning your return. Then, the runoff—you see a white man bathing in the desolate remains of a spring. Another israeli man is reading a newspaper. He sits on a boulder as if he doesn't know a house once stood there.

"This is the house where I grew up; that used to be the bakery downhill," Yacoub points onward as the rest of the class lags behind. In the distance, a building gapes like God smashed their fist down its frame in a tantrum.

As you near the hill's bottom, Yacoub points to the opposing hillside: "that hill—ya'ani—is where my father and his fathers were buried. The waste . . . Ya'ani . . . Sewage from Jerusalem runs down the hillside and erased his grave marker." You ask yourself: how many times has the state of israel asked Palestinians to marvel at their own land's suicide?

You reach the bottom. In the distance, there is a playground with a newly renovated park, speckles of white children running around. "The government started building a, a . . . Ya'ani, a new israeli quarter at the base of our village. This is our land, but they want to pave over it. We are fighting them, ya'ani, in the courts . . . But the construction has already begun."

On the way back, Yacoub points out a hybrid tree species that produces both almonds and berries. It is the result of decades of competition between an invasive species and a fruit gene indigenous to the region; two lineages, intertwined, refusing erasure. Science says that there are two likely outcomes to such speciation: either one species will conquer the other, or another entirely new species will emerge over generations. Yacoub calls it a genetic anomaly. A miracle of God.

# Elegy for the Birthright

*Church of the Holy Sepulchre, 2017*

from my parents, i inherited
my grandfather's gold cross—
country of cold metal—godless
in the land where God was man, once—

my grandfather's gold cross
gifted me security clearance; entry
into the land where God was man, once—
& the men are still machine-gun Gods

who gifted me security clearance; entry
to land not country enough to be home,
where the men are machine-gun God
-worshipers; at their expense, I inherited a new

land, not country enough to be
invisible, which turned my ancestors into God
-worshipers &, at their expense, I inherited a new God
whom I love like my country, & yet the closest i feel to Him

is in invisibility, to which my ancestors turned
when they inherited a new home, or Godless sanctuary
whom they loved like a country & yet the closest i felt
to my country was when touching my God's empty tomb—

who, in inheritance, left behind a Godless sanctuary
to echo the prayers He used to write for
my country, when in touch with God's empty;
permutations of familiar words, brief molar shadows

echoing in this sanctuary where He once wrote them,
& perhaps the prayer is in this dance of lip & limb,
permutations of familiar words, brief molar shadows,
as if my bones were chanting: *i was holy once*—

& perhaps that is the prayer; the dance of limb
i inherited from my parents, whose ancestors'
bones were chanting: *i was holy once*—
in this Godless country; *i was always holy*—

43

## in which you do not ask the state of israel to commit suicide

6 months later, you are back in your american college campus. A vial filled with Palestinian soil hangs on a strand around your neck. You feel it against your chest as you speak to the audience in their own language of proof and theorem.

You reference an equation from a paper in your hand and, as you glance down, re-notice TECHNION UNIVERSITY OF ISRAEL dominating the top of the page. "Their argument was a logical fallacy, so in a sense, the paper's authors cheated. They're israeli, so I suppose it makes sense."

You don't know why the words slip out of your mouth. And, for a second, time ceases to exist, and you are not a mere college student defending his thesis, but instead a Palestinian defending himself against a wall of petrified faces. Maybe it being "israeli Independence Day" weighed heavy on you. Or maybe every day is "israeli Independence Day," and your ancestors slipped out of your throat. Maybe it was the soil hanging from your neck like a key might; it is often the case that Palestinians who fled during the nakba still have the keys to their homes, even if they are no longer standing. In either case, there is always a mourning; there is always the lack of home placing a weight around your neck, a bullet in each word that escapes you.

A well-intentioned professor pulls you aside after your presentation and lectures you on professionalism. You want to tell him how Technion's existence is at the expense of your ancestor's land and lives, both of which they no longer have access to; how this same university makes an open-air laboratory of Gaza and calls them the *necessary expense*.

How, despite all of this, you are expected to sit docile as your own academic institution funds the crumble and rupture of your ancestral land. As if this same academic institution didn't turn their back when the Birthright campaign and other friends of israel threatened to put the Arab students on a watchlist. As if this same institution didn't try to swallow you into the night's mouth, tempting a moonlit suicide attempt from you, or that copy of you who craved most an escape that night.

Were you to die, would they write you into a boy on a godless ledge and speak not of the demons you fled or the gravity forming a hollow country in your heart? Or would they say you were just abandoning your body; would they say, "this is war, I mean, things like this just happen?"

But you are not the self you survived, nor are you the version of yourself who takes in words of the white professor who, you remind yourself, is well-intentioned. You are, instead, the copy of yourself you found at the entrance to the Aida refugee camp, 6 months prior, taking a selfie in front of a life-size statue of a key. While you are off being the literal Palestinian diasporic stereotype, your white classmates give candies to children walking in the streets and ask to take selfies with them. The children hold up 2 fingers next to their saviors in the photographs. #PeaceInTheMiddleEast on Instagram.

Inside the camp, a youth program director tells you about the role of art in the lives of the Palestinian refugee communities: "we began to notice our children were born into such desperate conditions that they dreamt of no other reality than becoming martyrs. It was our goal to teach our children that they could live for Palestine, too; that dying for their country wasn't their only future."

And at that point, all past, present, and future selves of you converge, as you ask again how many times the israeli state brought Palestinians to the brink of suicide; how the state instilled a learned helplessness in you; how the state molded you into the monster they always feared you to be, the monster you always feared in yourself. What of the self can exist outside a political rhetoric which, at best, will write you into something nonexistent?

## Letter to be Reflected and Thrown into the Shores of Tel Aviv

*after torrin a greathouse*

I am writing to you from a land where I am already myth. But I suppose you already knew that—you've seen it before, but not through my eyes. With nothing but the wind tethering you here from some other gone-ness you could imagine.

Let me be clear: to other men, this could be the right side of paradise. A foaming line waiting to swallow me back, where *where I came from* is no longer where I came from but, instead, a reckoning. Instead, a hunger I cannot afford. Oceanic. Only a queer thing can swallow that much and still remain a whole and single body. Desire is desire, and here I am, pooled and thirsting.

I promise, there is a distance when I call this *my capital* and they call it *theirs*, but there is also a distance when I call this *mine* and you, yours. It is a different kind of distance.

Here, our men don't have faces. Here, I've taken that blood-stained flag down, and yet, Palestinian is the only identity I've ever been certain about. I promise, there are men who want me, but cannot stomach the idea of me existing, even if you cannot imagine them.

Forgive me. I had such little faith in your imagination, but I'm beginning to think of faith as a fogged mirror, into which we look and witness ourselves outside of our selves. And, much like faith, we don't pray through mirrors; we understand through them. I want you to see me in this and every light:

I'm not asking you to imagine me, dead in a man's arms, but I am asking you to see me as always becoming, both I and the death of.

It's true. At the center of every myth is a loneliness larger than the whole of us. But is it not polyamory if I love myself into a multitude?

I'd like to think there is, somewhere, a *you* I can return to. I'm trying to say *I love you*, but I don't have the right mythos for it. I'm trying to say *I love him*, but he already isn't.

I don't want to call this a *coming out*. That would imply there was ever a border to reckon. If I let this become an elegy, that means I failed. War is war and war alone, and I don't want to speculate on all the exiles I could inherit at your hands.

I want to say I already forgive you for what is to come; that the opening wound of me forgives the ocean its salt, but this too is contingent upon the promise of violence.

Forgive me. I cannot fathom the concept of returning. I once imagined this as a letter to every person and country that once mothered me, but maybe I needed this to be a mirror:

This is what I know:

I fell in love with summer like it
                          wasn't
                    We kissed with all our
teeth.
He bit me and I liked it.              He bit me and the blood
                 surfaced but did not pool.
We pulled rivers from each other          until we forgot we were human.
We slow-danced in an empty field          as the world ended around us.
I am always on the edge of violence.          This is how I've constructed
mercy—          I mean, forgiveness is a sadness I cannot
afford—          I only know my lovers as seasons
that pass through me.          Therefore I am either land
or ocean          but never the border between—
I too want to be interrupted by daybreak.
I too have stained          and been stained beneath the same moonlight.
I'm not saying I love him,          I just want to be worthy of a good fight.
I promise, there are prettier ways to lie          to ourselves. Among ourselves.

You ask what the weather's like in my city every time. This is how you
understand distance. But what is an aubade but a lie we tell to
convince ourselves a bloodless morning is coming?

I loved him, phantasm. Forgive me.

I loved him, splendored & anthemless. Forgive us.

I lied. What I'm looking for is the opposite of forgiveness.

## Elegy in which the Birthright speaks back

*Outskirts of Jerusalem, 2017*

there is a voice behind
each morning prayer that wakes
Jerusalem before the rooster's
shrill cry—

       & before
it was a boisterous thing,
it was small; tiny itch
nestled between vocal cords,
brief settler—

       much like the heart
whose swelling cries, floods,
& tears membranes with its
wanting, & maybe wanting
is its own home—

       not the holy
vessel that begs its own rupture;
makes Jericho of its vast
chambers, tense with longing
of rivulet & fallow, almost
biological in its

       contradiction:
the body is holy
war enough for these
nations, swelling.
Brooding.

## in which you do not ask the state of israel to commit suicide

As you drive through the land, you can immediately discern which houses are Palestinian and which are israeli. Palestinian homes, not connected to israel's central water system, bear the mark and weight of water tanks, like lamb blood on a front door; as if the partition of water hasn't always been the difference between holy and crucified.

As they are written, israeli "zone laws" give the state legal control over the hilltops, aquifers, and other natural land resources in the West Bank. This is how the state writes Palestinian ethnic cleansing into "abandonment," hence "legal," hence "digestible."

You arrive at your destination: a small village in the central West Bank named Nabi Salih. Due to the natural resources surrounding the village, the state often sponsors "legal" home demolitions here: another suicide placed on your people's shoulders by the state.

For the past few years, the residents of Nabi Salih have been protesting the demolitions every Friday. A month before your arrival, you shared a viral video of a Palestinian teenager named Ahed Tamimi, who would often organize these protests. You saw her punch a soldier, who shot her cousin, square in the face. You saw her take history into her own hands with the sun in her hair. You called her a Hero.

She was recently taken from her bed in the middle of the night, her parents beaten half to death, and is currently being prosecuted in an israeli prison with her mother. The newspaper headlines talk of israelis holding barbeques outside of prisons housing Palestinians who are on a hunger strike. In case you were to forget the way they not only stole your land, but dance on it too.

In both resistance and compliance, your people are still asked to make a massacre of Home. As it is written, the history says you invited the soldiers and their tear gas into your living room. The history says children are often shot or injured in tear gas canister explosions. The history, as it is written, says this is still your fault; says your children suffered at the expense of your stubbornness.

The woman invites you into her rebuilt house and explains all of this to you, because you are not her; there is nothing connecting you but your stubborn blood, diluted, and the hyphenated American identity you inherited. Because you are not her, or Ahed Tamimi, or any other Palestinian taken into the night, you can write this testimony and, although it will never become History, it is a history nonetheless.

## Haifa Love Letters from a Palestinian Exile

i touched another
ocean today, love—let it
filter between my nail
bed shorelines & its sediment
stuck, stubborn, the way a lover's residue
stains & warms the wrong man's
bare skin—

      *

i want to tell you of a border
-less love: i found you at
the intersection of 5 countries, horizons
      bleeding into each other; here,
          there is enough history
     for the both of us, landlocked
         & gasping—what is love if not
an intertwining     of blood ?

      *

i left my heart in a sea
-glass sepulture & called it
home, fell in love with the brief
resurrections of it all—the shatters
& echoes of an empty tomb God left
us in—have you heard the good
news? have you seen your savior
in the streets today—empty
-palmed      & bleeding?

      *

i don't have trouble
with commitment—i just
don't know when i'll find love
again, so here i am: caught
between two lands not country
enough to be home, & neither
could ever love me    back—

*

Love, do not
tell me of
the bodies
you parted
to get here—
i know men
get lost
in the wholeness
of you & forget
what you swallowed
to pave
your ivory

*

you are not the God
i pray to, nor the mountain
& temples that robbed
Him—neither barbed-wire
eyebrow or cement jawline,
yours is a separation
unwritten, undressed—
        paradise *stolen*—
        paradise *reclaimed*—

*

& what of the breathless
martyrs—the ones who
tasted & trusted your waters
before it filled their lungs?

once, a lover asked,
*how do you see the ocean?*
& i meant to say, *i don't*
or, *only home*—

but said: *isn't living*
*for your country*
*just a slower way*
*to die?*

## in which you cannot ask the state of israel to commit suicide

After taking in your land, in history, in rupture, in song, you end your journey in Jaffa—a town on the Mediterranean coast, which was once the site of your grandparents' nostalgia. You strip to your bare skin and walk into the sea for the first, and last foreseeable, time.

You close your eyes and there is only quiet. A solemn quiet, but not a lonely one; these waters that no longer belong to you, cradling you in all your unfamiliar: the ghost of your grandfather's smile, his laughter waning like sunset; the ghost of your grandmother's baptism and her Jerusalem; the weight of all your everyones who could not exist here.

When all is done, you will go back to your country. You will retreat to western diplomacy and it will fail you. Again. You haven't a language in which this trauma is both digestible and reconcilable.

Suppose, instead, you began this by demanding the return of your land, even if it came at the expense of the israeli state. This means, you would be asking for the destruction of the state—yes, one that stole your home and forced death upon you—but the reality is, this narrative is never mentioned because this narrative has no language digestible to western diplomacy, hence no space to call its own. Your demands would, then, be labelled "a suicide," because they are always labelled "a suicide," despite all the suicides the israeli state has forced upon you. This would be the predictable ending; the ending your oppressor expects.

So, out of necessity in this framework, you do not ask the state of israel to commit suicide, because you cannot ask the state of israel to commit suicide. By choosing this path, your words become the ivory paving over Lifta, the tear gas canisters making a hollow echo of Nabi Salih, the steel-tipped boots of soldiers who first kicked your own grandparents out of their house. Your words ignore history at your own expense, and therefore, write you into something nonexistent.

In any case, you haven't a home to call your own, nor do you exist in a reality in which you can reclaim the home you deserve. Hence, you are told to rebuild, like your parents have rebuilt, survive like your ancestors have survived. And even that is its own type of amnesia: to rebuild home long enough to see your oppressor in its walls and eventually your own veins. Or escape. In any case, your oppressor has successfully engineered a reality in which you cannot see yourself existing.

Hence you arrive at your central contradiction: you exist, hence, you survived without a language to name that survival history. Hence, any attempt to give existing language to this would be to give your oppressor agency over your history, hence, write yourself out of History. To ask the oppressor to stop killing your people would be to ask the impossible; would be to beg wine out of a water that has failed you. Your ancestors have tried, time and time again. And failed.

Hence, you are trapped, by necessity, in this unsolvable binary between what is owed and what is realistic; between what is deserved and what is expected.

Proof that an equation is unsolvable in a given logical framework is of infinite value, compared to a solution damned to contradiction. What, exactly, can be achieved through this conception of *dialogue* when one side has two guns at their temple: one held up by the oppressor, the other held by their own selves.

In any case, the blood is always on your hands.

In any case, the blood is always your own.

# Cartographies of Light

*with thanks to Danez Smith, Delana Dameron,*
*Terrance Hayes & The Watering Hole 2017 Cohort*

*I. Miracle of Holy Fire (Church of the Holy Sepulchre, 162 CE)*

The angels overlooking Jerusalem are weeping light
rivers into goblets of wine & blood, over the body split
casual & made ritual of; the candle leaks itself, alit –
transfiguration of molten flesh resisting night.

In the sanctum, shapeless & blueing hues defy their plasmic
origin, praying not to human spectra to redefine their optic
censure; God's eye shining down upon his empty tomb
come prayerlight, come miracle & flicker of hollow womb.

Listen: the distinction between holy & heresy was always
a question of fire: the distinction between whore & saint lies
in who's burned for it – the distinction between martyr & false
god lies in whose testimony is set ablaze – the distinction
between Eden & exile lies in the tip of a sword on fire – my God,
a resurrection always to end in flames; holy, the fire refusing to burn –

*II. Brief Histories of Fire*

To resurrect us in flames, make holy the fire who refuses to burn
& un-name our geographies; call *city* a settlement & watch
that language char a home & syllable in one brief flash
& wound; because we have tasted its ash, death is a door
we refuse to walk through; we erect empty tombs to name it
contradiction; we build these & every heaven because we are greedy
to conquer eternity; because we watched our own dissolve
& slip through our grasp, we landlust & pray to countries
beyond our reach – because Jaffa is beautiful, it can't be
ours: the coastline flirts & begs crystal tithe; behind glass,
a gentrified hamsa cries & leaks moonlight; the air heavies
its timber beams as tendrils unravel beneath that humid – here,
an unfamiliar song fades into carved stone; here, a street cat
disappears into an endless alley & forgets its own reflection.

*

Into an endless alley, we disappear & forget our own reflections;

blame the fables for their brash amnesia: mirror, mirror
on the wall, whose country will be first to fall? Country,
country in our hearts, wherein does your allegiance build
contradiction? Where the roadway's pebbles skirt like sesame
from fresh kha'ik? Where the warmth of Saturday mornings can be
held in your hands; where khobzeh dissolves inflated plastic, vapors
& incense leaking into the air it inhabits; sometimes the city prays
without making a sound – a soldier peers into a vendor's stall &
empties the air; man bows to crumbling wall, & he is everyone's God.

In the old city, Teita's father punctures the throat of a persimmon,
spilling light before asking permission to touch & become that holy:

in america, Teita bites into the tiny sun in her palms & there
is no bloodshed: *in this country, not even the fruit translates –*

*

In no-country, the not-fruit untranslates its blood shed into
the bodyless lyric; that music without instrument – somewhere,
an unplucked lyre births a choir of angels from golden air;
somewhere a poem demands nothing to make a song of:
instead, the poem demands outline; instead of an out
-line, the corpse demands reliquaries & fills them too; instead
of each endlessly bodied night, may our every stolen town unghost –

instead of the net of kitchen scraps dangling above your head,
it was the neighboring street's silence that sang of decay. In Khalil,
arabic heavies the street as the settlers, from their heaven, bomb
-ard the arabic with newspaper, leftovers, sometimes acid; un
-dissolved, the hebrew graffiti reads *kill the arabs* bold & white
against dark stone; the ghost outline of Free          bleached to
its left; in this country, everything demands to be unwritten –

*

As it is left here, in this country, history demands to be unwritten:
the bus window's million particles coalesce, singular; the hell
-fire retreats back into that tiny-godded box; the arabic finds
small shelter in throat & palms, as the bus retches a man back
into country (not) stolen – footprints tracing back to a home
un-singular, as the wingless crane retracts from rubble; tears flow
north into pupils not yet dilated by flames, as bullets retreat back into
their tiny, tiny guns – as our homes rebuild themselves from thin air.

Not of dust, but hearth & golden hands; nights our words escape easy
as laughter. We fall in love, not with countries, but with how they leave
us breathless & without language; the mythos lying between a name &
its re-writing: a distance the size of a thousand exiles between *Al Quds*
& *Jerusalem, Khalil* & *Hebron;* no disappearing act: now you see it, now
you don't; a city doesn't just unbecome like that: a home doesn't just –

*

When our cities unbecome:  when our homes just    – & you don't,
because that was all this land demanded of you: survive & be
survived long enough to see your children plant their fists
beneath stubborn soil; tiny fists, small of earth; from birth, we
genetically inherit the mechanics of grasp – our first defense
mechanism being our closed fists, our biological resistance –
what of us wasn't meant to endure & be endured; we shed
& regrow a thousand cells each day from touch & small exiles:
come plow's lift, come well water; come rain, come tear gas;
come splintered frame, come cannister fire; come rubber, come
cased-bullet; come Nabi Salih, come nameless dead; come Arabic,
come no language; come soldier, come light flicker, come dark
dark room – come exile with the sun in her hair, come men always
men & night; come night, come forgotten gods, unmade & here –

*

That night, did the men & gods forget what they unmade
        to get here? Every unraveling, every sound unheard –
Everything that happened to us happened in a dark room;
        in the shadow of sunlight's abandonment, a planet's unheard
whimpers, yes & screams. & drought. We had our throats
        before those charred & desert landscapes sang, unheard –
The illusion of this country is in its fertility – we were never sand
        anything; we were farmers before every myth unheard –
Born with one foot already sworn to the soil; we were killed for this
        land, our bodies stolen & buried in this land, we were unheard
yes & un-listened to. The men who blued & flagged
        this state did so in violation of our unhearing –
Built border & checkpoint & stripsearch & door & gun to hide behind;
        nothing of their earth, wears a face outside of hellfire, unheard

*

Nothing of this earth wears our face; outside of hellfire,
we exist nowhere the trees don't uproot & become
us – the harpies, shrill-winged, pluck olives from us in cyclic

57

harvests; we speak only in the breakage. We never make a sound.
We forget ourselves in the screaming, when heavied by our own
shed flesh – even in divine speculation, we are burden in
existence. Even in death, this country still carries our name –
maybe every heaven is a Palestine we cannot inherit, so we pray
away its invisible; worship God even when He forgets our names,
our queer; the godless churches we write ourselves into, despite
every cross our ancestors bore to get us here: a house entombed
by wall on 3 sides, bleached & undecorated of its ink, aside
from a lone bird – maybe that bird is a God we can have
faith in to become human – to make & escape every labyrinth.

III. *The Apartheid Wall Writes your Suicide Note*
*– a cento of graffiti from the israeli apartheid wall*

IN MY PREVIOUS LIFE    I WAS HUMAN    WITH FAITH I MADE    A LABYRINTH
OF MYSELF    & BURNED    FOREVER I REMAINED    IN EXISTENCE    GOD  OF EYES
UNOPENED    NO CONSCIOUSNESS JUST    EXISTENCE WITHOUT    THEY TOLD US
TO EXIST IS TO RESIST    THE PALESTINIAN SPIRIT IS STRONGER    THAN ANY

COUNTRY    YOU MUST RIOT    TO BE HEARD    A LIE I CANNOT LIVE    THE TRUTH BEING
WE ARE ALL WAITING    FOR DEATH HOPE IS    A TERRITORY I AM ASHAMED TO LIVE IN
HOW SOON DO WE FORGET    TO OPEN HEARTS  AT ALL COSTS    THE HANDS
THAT BUILD CAN ALSO TEAR    THROUGH DEATH  & DISCOVER THE ASHES    OF SELF
BEAUTY    A MIRROR    WHERE SENSELESS    OBJECTS FAIL TO    REFLECT

CUT AWAY THE POISONED    YESTERDAYS A COUNTRY IS NOT    ONLY WHAT IT DOES
BUT WHAT IT TOLERATES    I AM ASHAMED TO LIVE    IN A WORLD THAT BUILT ME

IF THERE IS TO BE A HEAVEN    LET IT BE THE COUNTRY    I RETURN TO STONE    OF HOPE
IN A MIGHTY STREAM    OF ASH    & TEARS JESUS WEPT    FOR JERUSALEM LET ME
FALL INTO    THOSE INCOMPLETE & FAMILIAR    WATERS    I WAS BETTER THERE

IV. *Maqam: Sunlight Speaks to the Children of Exile*

Fall rains incomplete & familiar waters – you were better there,
where the clouds are heavy with your name again. In america,
they will call this season beautiful & you will learn to marvel
as the dead dance, mid-air, in winded suicides; everything alive
around you, withering; the leaves bleeding into a watercolor wind,
as if to say, "God – carry us, weightless, to a land we could
Return to." But I shine on no God; I cannot dissolve the opaque
turbulence that grows heavy between us, even with light
overlooking this endless ocean; home that beckons
your return in solar eruption, swelling daylight; cirrhus
of ionized dust, of chaotic plasma trajectory, when I am most

distant from the wreckage of planets – this, our smolder,
inherited. Our inferno, our godless bodies drifting in vast,
endless empty – unpromised, sailing between moon & star –

*

When endless emptiness unpromised us moon & star,
the way man unpromises body & colonizer unpromises land
ensuing the genocide & erratic mercury, did they forget we know
what it means to set ourselves ablaze to keep an unforgiving nation
alive? We of trembling plasma & superheated vaporization –
how countries shield themselves from our flares & thrashes as if
this brilliant combustion wasn't the reason they breathe – did they
think us saviors? I have never been a forgiving god,
and neither are you; though you do carry the weight of a thousand
galaxies, so it follows that you are, in fact, the horizon itself –
yes, sometimes we lose ourselves in the noiseless rush of dying
starlight, of patient dust; this eternity of elliptical dancing,
breathless in repetition, damned to cyclic & inherited implosion –

*

Breathless & stellar, we are damned to cyclic & inherited implosion
because we were nothing less than heavenly beings, swallowed
by ceaseless night. Yes, there are days you'll curse the universe
its peculiar gravity; how we chase ourselves up, ceaselessly,
from another oblivion, as if our organs weren't drifting
continents; as if we loved our bodies in a way we can never love
a country – the invisible hues of ourselves, leaking unto galaxy
the way paint graffities apartheid wall or bullet makes epitaph
of an already forgotten saint, whom you begat the heavens of,
in wake. Because your lineage has quaked in its shadow, let this not
be song of winter & its cold metallic embrace like that of gun,
of black hole's ceaseless entropy; let this not be a metaphor
for bleeding sun or falsetto wisps peaking over horizon; let it sing
to every land, earthed & unearthed: troubled yet fallow –

*

& to that land unearthed, troubled yet fallow,
            I sing praise to your rewritten & eroded topography –
To hands that plow & seed a forgotten history,
            I sing praise to your calloused & unwounded exterior –
To soil that cradles everything, even in betrayal,
            I sing praise to the weight you swallow & inhabit –
I know somewhere, the land sings love to its people

59

the way street cat howls to moonlight
in lonesome gaze; somewhere, I kiss the Mediterranean
                    & no one drowns at the intersection of salt & fury;
somewhere, a patient God holds the universe
                        with our tiny bodies, ravaging in his arms;
somewhere, our children wake up & become music
                    like dabke was just another word for morning prayer

                    *

            & dabke was not another word        for mourning –
        how, even in death     our people are always     waking
                music – are always     guttural melody        thickening the air's
        hot empty – are always        trespassers who danced     on holy
            land –        wine before water       emptied & transfigured
        us into          communion –               backwards miracle,
    of ungodly magic –        deity of backfired         apocalypse, we tore
        down the Earth       & called it ceremony     so today, I call us
        counterpoint, call us     God   -swallowers; dissonance     without
            sacrament – choir of unholy  amnesia: we believe in      earth's end
    because we survived it –     children of the waking     damned, of grace
    -less falsetto    it was our bones    that split the oppressor's     fracturing
        hands: of second sun – of rising  Filasteen –    in refusing collision,
    we resurrect ourselves    from God's lungs   & burn   & sing    again –

*V. Ascension*

In refusing collision, we are resurrected from God's lungs & burning
landscapes, come eagle's clasp & angel's palm; we've spent lifetimes
searching for a light to bend towards & outwrite our names from
every unending & darkening trajectory – the qahwa grinds, coalescing
& upturned; the cartographies of every palm, arched & crossing.
We've bordered the countries into our hands, yet our every writing of
death is always a skyward hurl; an escape of wings & never a water
-lily lullaby; as if our heaven was not a golden-gated country
but a map not drawn in wall with no waters to cross us – a here
without a need for bodies; we already survived that – maybe God
loved us so much, he had to keep us in arms' reach; until the flowers
don't demand our veins' honeyed nectar; until we don't have to craft
divinity in mirrored tongues to survive & be worth surviving; until
the angels of Jerusalem can look upon us, in full bloom, weeping light.

# III. Adaptation

"& what is a country but the drawing of a line?
I draw black lines around my eyes & they are a country . . .
& for every country I lose, I make another & make another"
—Safia Elhillo

## *from* Adaptation Portraits (strange cartographies)

A Truth about displacement:
most of my ancestors lived
unremarkable lives. Before
he was my grandfather, he was a boy
who laughed at echoing hand
farts with his cousins, mocked
Shakespeare & his silly english
in school, pissed off all the teachers
between cigarette smoke—

Nabil remembers it like this:
instead of getting jumped, he beat up
all 8 of the older boys
who cornered him on the playground
& that's the story of resilience

before Palestinians woke up
in a different country. Not all of us
were kicked out by brute force
& iron boot. Though all were

displaced. Some were lucky enough
to see the writing on the wall
before the wall existed; to wake up
to a less swollen sun, bite into
that same unremarkable
fruit every morning—

                    (

A Truth about displacement:
i once burned an american
flag & a white nationalist
threatened to kill me.

A brown boy said
*Free Palestine* & a white nationalist threatened
his whole family. & you already know
which one the FBI visited—

you already know
how this story ends—

(

My cousin, the lawyer, tells me,
*we're american, so we're friends
of israel now.* He used
the word *democracy* several times
& his tongue didn't
reject it.

Every line from the cartographer's pen
draws a red-stained atlas, hostiles
the landscape until it is
our blood—

this is how a country levels
every genome into white—

(

Evolution study:
  Palestinian man wakes up
  in america & forgets
   himself—

Evolution study:
  humanoid species adapts to strange
  cartography & ascends
   the food chain.

(

Once, i came out
as non-binary & a Palestinian man
looked right through me.

He was queer. Painted us
lone islands in all that
ocean & I have since known
queerness to be weapon more than
identity politic—in the hands of men
anything can be a border
if you try hard enough,

even bodies—the line
where cell meets wall—
the line where hand meets
rupturing chest—

where a pair of unwanted lips
leave a dull etching
of an unnamed country
on my cheek—

(

A Truth about our bodies:
the limbic system, control center
for emotion & memory, is named
from the latin *limbus*, meaning
*border*, meaning:
        every memory is a border
        drawn in limbs—
meaning:
        this is where I am defined
        & so my gender must live

there—at a border,
always on the verge
of bursting—

to ask for a framework
for understanding our bodies
that doesn't rely on borders
& the implicit binaries therein—

Let me disrespect your language
with my being: every man
has betrayed & untranslated me
in the same way
this country has.

(

I wonder what nakba meant before
1948. Or if it even existed.

Some say it was used decades before,
in the context of Pan-Syrian diasporas.

Or maybe history birthed a word
to call nakba to call Palestine to call
memory of & now, you cannot
look at me or my country & not
think *catastrophe*—

& I can't forgive israelis
for that. Or americans.

How can anyone afford
forgiveness in a time like this?

(

A Truth about my dispossession:
the second time I did not
kill myself, I swore I'd be
more generous to my body,
but, for accountability's sake, I confess
that, some nights, the open window speaks
back to me & calls itself *inheritance*—

this being the cartography
of concrete split between map
& memory—

you win, america.
I've inherited your fear
of heights—conditioned myself
to shudder at the thought
of me most nights
I nod to sleep anyways
tell myself it was nothing
nothing but the wind
perhaps

yes.

the wind. it was
the wind. it was
only the wind.

## Ekphrasis

in another universe i grow up
to want and be wanted whole
with the concave flux of rainbow flags
in the wind like lapsing waves

in this city my mother's family build
between the flash and rush of trolleys
both heard and unheard

my mother wasn't a metaphor for drowning
yet here she could be
the immigrant daughter playing Galaga
at her father's store
with the whole universe in her hands

i believe this to be an inheritance
because Tel Aviv slipped through our grasp
sometimes history makes a repetition of us

from this hilltop you can see the ocean
perhaps this was all my mother wanted:
to look into the horizon,
see her own reflection
with her own blood

## on Mirror Skylines

somewhere i could inherit safety
and not at my own expense
the flags of stolen nations rippling
in synchronous blood-fall

themselves a sanctuary
above bellowing earth
the story goes

on this mirrored shoreline
my mother illuminated
between counted and dirt-stained quarters
from which she was displaced
lost country, forgotten mountainside

we cannot escape
we plant into another land uprooted
sometimes we make a repetition of history

consume the whole skyline
to survive another day without drowning
brute, unbridled, and not
among the waves shimmering
indistinguishable amidst the refracting light

# To All the Ghosts I've Loved Before
*A Palinode in 15 Unsent Valentines*

My heart is driving through a field in Maine. Her opening
scene is yellowed with grief, & this is the first time
she thinks of you all week. Most of america is dead
landscape, & here, when she must confront this emptying,
vulnerable planet, she wonders how Jupiter can exist without
a surface – as sphere compacted in gas bound only by the gravity
of a dense molten core – how somewhere in the universe, stability
exists in the midst of soundless fire without land to ground it –

\*

Loneliness Is a high school gym floor: scene where we're both single
at homecoming, & I lean into you; say, *maybe we can find boys to dance with
instead*. You laugh with and not at me. In truth, I just want to be held –

\*

*Killing it,* you say; your hand grazing my velvet top –
scene where all the straight boys can't keep their hands off
me – scene where I am vast and un-controllable, held
by everyone and no one in that blue – I am never
       last to leave     any party.

\*

Me, I Must be kidding myself? Scene where a girl, whose name
I can't remember, crowns you in plastic on a football field, kisses
your cheek; whereas you're the only one I'd go to that field
for – scene where I'm crying while that All-American
Rejects album (you know the one) blares the whole drive back,
      & the mascara practically writes itself down my face –

\*

Confess(ion): I'm starting to think I have an attraction to
impossibility – tonight, the sky is a punched-out molar,
& here I imagine a desire vast enough to bleed & float for –
when you text me *i love you,* i drift to sleep & leave you on *seen*

\*

I Still the blades in every dreamscape that night:
      still life in empty field commemorating the absence of fire –

still life with dandelions, mid-eruption, parading nowhere –
still life with lone daffodil slow-dancing with the space
        around it – observe its antiphysic: say, instead, every
        motion was shaped & guided not by limb but the air
        around it – what is gravity if not the loneliest ancestor
        rejecting the very notion    of sky?

*

Believe        (me when I say a poem can
      be unforgiveable. Watch as I break
      the poem, unforgiveable. Every line
      a breakage and, by construction, unforgiveable)
Still; Believe    ( me, I can redact the air
      by my unforgiving. I have never left
      a poem anything but unforgiven. )

*

When I'm Not With You I     Lose    nothing – & those truths
scare me sometimes. You            married a nice girl
beneath a dead & autumned tree      to prove a point.
*To whom,* I wonder. I do not ask     how she fissured
your heart into twin countries.      I'm trying to be
happy for you. I'm trying        to be happy for.

*

My Mind isn't always this generous. By this time
next year, I'll have spent more time on earth loving you than not
        knowing of your existence –

*

Give Me something? A memory, like Adele asked for?
Let me be a selfish for a minute; I need to
construct a chest to fold into & define love in
the collapse of me, & sure, that is not unlike memory:
        to want not you but a needing of –
        Forgive me. I'm not asking for forgiveness.

*

A Sign of healing: the last time a white boy begged for me, cornfields
swallowed the horizon, aside from the line the highway makes
when it waltzes into the sun  in crooked rhythm –   I brought myself

to climax, walked into his room, & burst before he even opened
his mouth. I was Hot because I was          untouchable, for once: scene
        where I conquered impossibility –          became it –
showed him none of me was intended      for him –        & his –

                              *

Hit Me / like the brakes / you never wanted / to press down / that /
bend at that / speed polevault me / into a lackluster / lover exhaust /
me into serenade & / surrender / disrespect me / like a run-on
/ sentence what's the point / of want / if it isn't / full-throttle beg /
for me & I'll call you / air I want you / to breathe / me.

                              *

*Baby,* One word for you that never felt comfortable
In my mouth, despite the synonyms for you: *babe, bb, be*
*-eb,habib* – *baby* is a boring I cannot afford. Give me
a queer love so mundane it doesn't have to kill me –

                              *

More the flocking of sparrows, less the drifting of –

You ever look into a man & see a wilderness? You ever
look into a wilderness & see fire? Soot & eyeline. This
& every ecosystem could exist as fine without us:

        see the dandelions shedding tiny countries adrift
                nowhere? See the daffodils, wide-mouthed,
                        unbecoming, that    & everywhere?

                              *

Time as a final locus of and against control:
time as not-space, as elegy's sprawling: admit it –
we all need a framework of anti-mirror:

                I have never looked into a love song & seen myself.
                Every poem I enter leaves me seen & anything
                but. Listen: I am trying to tell you a story about distance.

# ars poetica with waning memory
*after Tarfia Faizullah and Vievee Francis*

there was a dead tree rotting behind the church
over there. & wedding bells. they danced. or was it collision
i wanted. the pianist's misstruck chords. a false minor.
he asked what my hands could do. he called me
a dog. it was a joke. he dropped the dog. then kissed it. he wanted
me. an *it* he joked about raping. because he could not
admit. it happened. the basement. there. the lights
flickering. until they weren't. an inhabited dark. burnt
their soft coils. i didn't want to. see. anything. his hand sliding
beneath me. pretending he wanted me. to cum. i came
on my own accord. i was never there. my stain, a small country
he didn't notice. i, a small country on his couch. i fled.
i thanked him. on the way out. that language without
voice. that body without. dead tree. a rotting.
a man was here once. i plucked the instrument until
no man. o tenor hum. o vibrato of shedding dead.
yes i touched the copper-gutted socket. there was a puddle
5 inches to my left. were it a larger stain i would have unbroken
that circuit &. a light. alight. i flicker. & am
no longer. i touched a white man. once. i do not touch white men
like that. men who touch me like rotting tree. men who fuck me into
dead country. stain on rubble. stain on earthly stain. there were trees
here once. those men's hands stained with its gold. an ethnic
cleansing. i touch myself & do not leak gold. i touch myself. there.
the mind craves. the body cannot. i synapse & closed circuit. desire's
molecular inception, i. expulsion of spinning orbitals. the mind's
momentum, electric. until i cannot be. until i red
& leak. wound un-cauterized. i've killed myself many times. i haven't
died yet. i've died for men. many times. they do not call me
savior. i don't know this song. the words don't translate. the melody,
a pianist's trembling hands. or was it dancing. i familiar the wind.
that wind, a kind of language. i could touch. the language escaped me.

## Essay on Submission

Having ebbed in the disbelief of it instead of its weight.

Stone-tiled the floor the blood a trickling fire.

Confessional here the ocean metaphor.

Refused he tore me shut & seeping no.

Vastness to marvel or hide.

In being told i don't exist i laugh with wounded teeth into.

The folds of his larynx a choir of bees rattle me.

Into myth less the mechanics of.

Throat than the usage the context neither divorced from combustion.

Of birth more or less i forgave him before.

He entered because he swelled for me i could never trust.

Myself in his hands but i did want.

Him.

Knocking leaning into the sliver of light a peeled condom.

Missed the wastebasket he couldn't bear.

The sight of me i never slept.

With the lights off i don't know that.

Story.

But i named it so it can't be.

Holy.

Or rather question of.

Distance my skin and.

Cold waters my skin and woundless.

Skin i wade in the contradiction.

After i wanted only to be.

Held.

No.

Distance his hand & the small of my.

Back his hand & the lip.

Of a waterfall here i reject the landscape.

Its vastness i don't think.

We're looking for the same thing you.

And i you'd think olympus.

Would dethrone itself of goldenrod leaves i told you it was.

Blood did i claim it.

Mine i am built of avoidable.

Violences with one drop apocalypse.

The burning wilderness you can see yourself.

Out now histories like this cannot.

Be known let alone escaped even the one.

Where i set fire to my colonizer i can afford neither.

Reclamation nor reconciliation.

No.

Unfragmented i cannot give you an ending.

That isn't lunar and.

Concave staining instead.

The bathroom floor.

# alternate mythologies of vengeance, in fragments

*The video game,* Assassin's Creed: Origins, *follows an ancient Egyptian assassin named Bayak, and his wife Aya, who work to protect the people under Ptolemy XIII's rule. Their son was martyred by the Ptolemic police state, and so the game follows Bayak and Aya's quest to dismantle the entire state via a chain of assassinations.*

---

or was i the wind          that sang the river     -bed into gentle
  quiet & not      the doe whose stone  -soft tongue   could trust
  that water?                    or was i

         the parted flesh        which lies   nerveless
between cartilage       & skin         beneath the nose's wide bridge
& not  the steel      that pierced it?           that i could altar

        my topology              & not      forget my former
shell—     that i could unbecome       with nail & steel without
perishing in the crucifixion—      when i bleed   i bleed    soft
     as stone's ripple    & it is tame— unrevolutionary
in leak—that i could even      witness myself outside of my    self—

*

a stranger calls me  *militant* says  *smile for the picture, you look like you could kill someone* like she forgot     our gods razed temples   before we wrote them
into patient—    a white woman says
       *you were tender   once* & that          is her imagined
holy—my aunt sees steel    in my nostril    asks if i've forgotten
my roots & that           is a holy         she clings to—i set fire
in another        stranger's mouth & that          is a holy i run from—

*

     suppose the stranger's mouth was      instead    a country
who birthed me    in swaddling   ash & dared call me       ungrateful—

       suppose   instead i run—   & split
cities    in my graceless path     like it was instinct—

*

                                                        i saw a man
who set fire     to me    before     in the reflection     of a glass window
& i       wasn't i    fled before processing     the ghost i witnessed—
                 in another          reality i would          smile like i smile
at weddings          while burning     history or
                              i would quench          my fists who wanted
to wear him          crimson     & in truth both          realities scared me
in truth i saw          too much of myself          in every reflection   & so i
fled—& so i          soft          my own defense mechanism—

                                        *


in the game a mxn     with skin-thick beard scales     the Alexandria skyline
in search          of men     & i find him          beautiful i find him     funeral
    laughter—or          middle finger to security          camera—for what is
an ancestor          if not a mxn          in the sky with a wound
          for a heart—     if not tantrum     of stone & ricochet—a hunt
for false gods     in a dark we could bleed          into     & become—
          here is a heart          screaming—     a blade—     a blade—
a puncture—     here he is anything but          sacrifice until
that knife—     the work being his          own—this wound being his—
                              say that knife was
instead a police     state—say his boy     with that knife in his heart
was a wound     no—     his boy     was a wound     in his heart
like a knife & so          he flies & so
                              he softs the bloodshed—slices
the air &                         3 bodies—          night pooling
onto pavement     in a winded dance          of silenced feet & bless
those hands          who pulverize the skulls          of man with remnants
of their crumbling
                         citadels—the hands          who hunt not
the men          who martyred but the state          who birthed them
crimson—for God     so loved     that boy He took him     onto cliff's edge
               & dared him
                         to jump—
                                        & is that not the holiest
                                        love—a love you must
survive for—a love     that dissolves          countries—i'd like to think
i too was descendent     of a softness     that could shatter     bones—

                                        *


how history says most suicide bombers during the intifada


                                        77

                              were victims      of home demolitions—
how history tells me all i know of resistance
                                 is a flight      of stubborn blood—


                        *


how history says my teita fled    on foot to Egypt     while pregnant
so her son didn't have to be born        in exile—i want to call this
            an act of resistance        but i can only know it as softness—
      when the skies birthed their blood
                        -ied sandstorms—    when the IDF held a machine gun
                                                      to her womb—


            the kind of love you'd betray      a country for—


                        *


my sido's golden tear     -ducts the night      his son was born
    in swaddling cloth                  in a country      he did not belong to—


                  my father          his fists      crumbling walls
                                      the night i first      left—


      a doe leaps out      into my brother's headlights
              & he swerves          wrecks himself        to avoid
                                            the bloodshed—
                        *


                  i hug the woman          who married the first boy
            i ever loved      & smile—say    *i'm happy*
*for you*        because i couldn't        set fire      to another man
    not tonight              so i dance        like i mean it i dance
& my feet        pass over the ghosts      of a thousand embers—i inhale
the smoke— his trembling      wedding vow—an unhinged
    door frame   a hand   a hand          a quenching        light—
a window          a man          his night—        or was it    mine—
    the parking lot          a mouth          i unzip    set fire
i do not stay—    i am already mid          -flight—a TSA officer's hand
    to my groin—      much like   a wedding    vow i swear    i saw him
t r e m b l i n g   yes—a love    like stolen    countries—no    a dance i
dance i   dance i was just          dancing          i was just—
    *i don't think      we're looking for the same thing you          & i—*
    *i mean*          i was just          dancing—


                        78

# CARTOGRAPHIES OF WIND
*An Exhibition*

*Inscription:*

Here, the archive will be held accountable for the bodies taken, at its expense. This is how existence is written into contradiction. In truth, my work thus far has centered around these violences and the central contradiction that Palestinian voices are both systemically silenced and only digestible in their pain. Which the archive writes into both cyclic and inescapable.

In truth, much of my family survived. Because they were in Ramallah. At the right time. What of the Palestine that did not make it? The villages written into abandoned. Whose remains give way to overgrowth & bleeding foliage. Here, life will be held accountable for the death it paves over. In truth, these landscapes, after becoming the site of mass expulsion, rape, and massacre, have been repeatedly violated. Men now shoot porn scenes over this rubble. Now build condos over this rubble. Children now laugh on playgrounds built over this rubble. Before it was rubble, it was house & home & bakery & olive press & water & wells hand-dug & kha'ik shedding sesame seeds like summer rain & life & life & life & life &.

Can I write about Palestine without writing of its erasure? Can Palestine exist in the space outside of its negative, outside of the trauma we are told is both cyclic and inescapable? Does the archive have the capacity to avenge these bodies, the land, & the bond between them?

I do not have access to pre-1948 Palestine. The landscape has been desecrated. Irreversibly so in some respects.

And yet, I can't help but see Palestine. Everywhere.

## After Balfour

the achievement of
a national home in
sympathy

this object

      *

I have much pleasure in conveying to you
this object

it being     that nothing   in Palestine
has been
clearly understood

      *

I should be grateful     for the
declaration of sympathy    of a national home
which has been submitted
on behalf of    existing non-Jewish communities in Palestine

      *

the achievement of
a national home    in
nothing

      *

I have much pleasure in con

of a national home

      *

the achievement of
a national home    for
nothing

\*

I should be grateful
that     nothing
has been
country

\*

a national home
shall be
religious
pleasure

\*

Palestine

this object
of country

\*

establishment
of   pleasure

this object
has been
submitted

\*

It being     nothing
that   I should be grateful     for

\*

pleasure

submitted

clearly understood.

# Annihilation Landscapes

In the movie *Annihilation*, an Eden-like land known as Area X radiates from the coast, expanding and eventually swallowing cities under a force-field known as the Shimmer, which refracts DNA sequences and mutates all life into a continuum of hybrid species. Examples of mutated species include a bear absorbing the human voice of its last victim's dying moments and trees made of salt sprouting on the shoreline. The following are a series of landscapes and mutations from the film, as explored by the main characters, including a biologist, a psychologist, a medic, a linguist, and a physicist.

### I. Still Life of Abandoned Village

> instead of a body, a vine
> > threading itself into fractal twirl—
>
> tendrils like endless fingers, reaching
> > for child, spat up from soil & root—
>
> a continuum of rosebuds blooming
> > from the exit wounds, say
>
> they write themselves into casket
> > hollow—find life blooming
>
> in every absence; but do not say
> > they abandoned their bodies
>
> in this country of nameless wind—
> > i cannot look at them & not see Palestine—

### II. Still Life in the Mouth of Bear with Stolen Voice

*& beneath those jaws*     *a tongue to call*

*human*          *the voice*

*beast* *-throated*

*box splitmouth*     *splitsilenced*

*can i*   *write silent*    *without*    *unfleshing*   *history takes*

*no victims*    *writes victim*    *into* DNA    *morphology of*

*bodied*   *night*   *sometimes we*    *splitmap*   *we unbecome*

*our cartographies*  *& unsee*   *those mouths*    *their ripping*

*of flesh*  *i cannot write*    *history*    *without blood*   *tied*

*hands*   *i exhale*    *wound*    *if i survive*

*as victimsong*    *did that voice*    *ever belong*    *in my mouth*

*i swallowing*    *eternal my*    *rupture*   *-d chords*

*i void*    *an eternity*    *of shapeless*    *screaming*

HELP ME: HELP: HELP: HELP ME: HELP: HELP:
HELP : HELP ME : HELP : HELP : HELP ME : HELP:

*(background refrain repeated throughout: HELP ME: HELP: HELP ME: HELP:)*

*III. Still Life of Shoreline with Salt Trees*

here            ion, the sea       eviscerate
the tree        's spine           d, digest
s shatter       ed glass           ed whole
into scabs      & wreck            the branches
& eros          nerves crash       have teeth
                electric in        shore's edge
                stead of           a rest
                a palm             less jaw
                a rib              line here
                                   a his
                                   story writ
                                   ten in
                                   fracture


*IV. Still Life with the Physicist's Scarred Forearms*

you have seen the jawbone erupt into ambrosia
clouds & escape from skull in flowered exit wounds—

you have seen the ribcage turned vine rivulet, survived
the water lillied pillows, plucked from our refracted matter
before you swore you housed an expanding genome—

you knew self-detonation's song before nature mothered
you into everything & nothing all at once—the ghosts
of a thousand knives blooming inside that earth-still
skin; i confess, i too have dreamt myself flowered

in death; annihilation was the easiest story i could write
of myself; i immerse myself in refracted rivers, of chalk
& blackboard—i construct arcadias to forget myself

in every framework; yes, every mythos of self is a suicide
mission by construction—sometimes, the most violent
destinies are written in the gardener's palms—

here, every vine & root demands blood—
here, every life is birthed from hollow absence—

# Ekphrasis with Toothing Chainsaw in Unnamed Halhul Vineyard
*a Markov Sonnet*

The waraq, empty of chlorophyll, hung chewed & dangling
Because there was no witness amidst the yellowing foliage.
The toothing beast's rapture, heavy in the air like a song.

*\*\*\**

Because there was no witness amidst the yellowing foliage,
The toothing beast's rapture, heavy in the air like a song
Unfamiliar to soil-worn hands, harvesting small implosions.

*\*\*\**

The toothing beast's rapture, heavy in the air like a song
Unfamiliar to soil-worn hands. Harvesting small implosions,
A marble heaven built over hill & tomb, reaches everywhere.

*\*\*\**

Unfamiliar to soil-worn hands harvesting small implosions,
A marble heaven built over hill & tomb reaches everywhere
The unyellowed, muting wind can neither stain nor uproot.

*\*\*\**

A marble heaven built over hill & tomb reaches everywhere.
The unyellowed, muting wind can neither stain nor uproot
A land ungodded—the dead's hollow, hallowed roaring.

*\*\*\**

The unyellowed, muting wind can neither stain nor uproot
A land ungodded. The dead's hollow, hallowed roaring
Silence, interrupted by riot of metal teeth & ricochet.

*\*\*\**

A land ungodded the dead's hollow, hallowed roaring
Silence. Interrupted by riot of metal teeth & ricochet,
A country can only be accountable for the screams.

Silence interrupted by riot of metal teeth & ricochet.
A country can only be accountable for the screams
We cannot unhear or unwrite from our memory.

\*\*\*

A country can only be accountable for the screams
We cannot unhear. Or unwrite from our memory,
A history unfragmented, free of limbs disfigured.

\*\*\*

We cannot unhear or unwrite, from our memory,
A history unfragmented. Free of limbs disfigured,
Would you believe me if I said I bled for this?

\*\*\*

A history unfragmented, free of limbs. Disfigured,
Would you believe me if I said I bled for this?
Leaves caught in my throat like a contradiction.

\*\*\*

Would you believe me if I said I bled for this—
Leaves caught in my throat like a contradiction:
*Name name name unname name—    name name name unname name—*

\*\*\*

Leaves caught in my throat like a contradiction:
*Name name name unname name—    name name name unname* name
The waraq, empty of chlorophyll, hung chewed & dangling.

\*\*\*

*Name name name unname name—    name name name unname name—*
The waraq, empty of chlorophyll, hung chewed & dangling
Because there was no witness amidst the yellowing foliage.

## Ekphrasis on a Fragmented Nationalism

Somewhere in Tel Aviv, israeli "citizens" are walking through an art exhibition called *Stolen Arab Art*. This is not a metaphor—the show features four unattributed video art installations created by (Arab) artists, without the consent of those (Arab) artists.

Here, (Arab) is a placeholder for Palestinian, but I suppose that goes without saying. In every interview, the curator (an israeli who is not Palestinian) defends the installation as a comment against the cultural boycott of the zionist state, claiming the exhibition is a "performative action," hence all visitors are performers, and everyone—curators, attendees, artists—is implicated in the theft.

In a way, the curator is correct: at the center of all settler colonial projects is theft. All interactions with the settler colonial project, cultural or economic, normalize the existence of the aforementioned settler colonial project, which, again, is contingent upon theft by construction. The premise of the installation is, therefore, a contradiction, much like the zionist state: the curator, intending to criticize boycotts of the zionist state, perpetuates the precise colonial theft being criticized.

Somewhere in Tel Aviv, an israeli "citizen" is reading a book titled *Huriya*, which translates to "freedom" in Arabic. In 2018, an israeli publisher collected, translated, and published this series of essays by (Arab) women without their consent, to be sold as "freedom" to the people occupying (Arab) land. The metaphor is self-evident. Unsurprising. Within the walls of an exhibition and the pages of a book, israelis dare imagine works of Palestinian imagination as their own & isn't that how this all began?

The blueprint of the zionist project was once a drop of ink on papers mandating a project whose enactment occurred at the Palestinians' expense. The founders of the zionist project imagined Palestinians as invalid occupants, imagined into voluntary exiles on the wrong end of a (two-sided) war, imagined into nonexistent.

Nationalism is not unlike art in this separation between subject and perception of—imagination being the link between the two. This is how the colonial imagination survives. Festers. *Stolen Arab Art* could never exist without (Arab) art. The distinction between the two is not unlike the distinction between Palestine and occupied Palestine: the colonizers imagined ownership through a framework in which that ownership was not only convenient but already assumed.

*

To this day, I still know by heart the lyrics to every song of my Southern childhood, every convenient depiction of the american project. Every *one nation under god* punctuated by a lyric portrait: *from the lakes of Minnesota to the hills of Tennessee, sweet land of liberty, from sea to shining sea.* This was the daily routine of my early upbringing—what reason did a seven-year-old have to question what, exactly, the seas were shining with?

Palestine was a word conveniently missing from my lexicon, but labneh wasn't. Or falafel. Or sfiha or khazanah. My household Arabic was the only thing that set me apart from my other classmates, and for that reason, it was our family's biggest secret. Any whisper outside the house was accompanied by a quick translation. Every khobzeh turned into bread, every jibneh, a tired cheddar.

I first heard the word Palestine in second grade, when I was assigned a project on family history. When my mother first said it, I went to my globe but could not find it anywhere. I thought to myself, "she must have meant Pakistan," because it was the most similar name I could find. When I gave a presentation about my Pakistani family heritage and our falafel, I garnered many confused looks from my classmates.

"israel. The land that the Bible calls israel. That's where we're from," my mother told me after school that day. What else was she supposed to say to me, after hearing that my friend's family came from a country shaped like a boot, and that the new student transferred in from a faraway constellation of islands? How exactly was she meant to describe the shape of thin air to her son, who spoke only the clumsiest Arabic?

And such is the colonial imagination: we didn't need to miss the roaming hills of Palestine because we had the american mountainside. We pledged allegiance to this land every day, and so it became ours. We are reminded that men died for that flag of stars, and so this land is ours. We ate our turkey and green bean casserole. We learned to give thanks and shut the fuck up.

*

Summer 2016: I was living in New York City for the first time, after finishing my worst semester—a semester that, as you may recall, almost took my life. That summer was when I first discovered *Hamilton* & became obsessed: listening to the soundtrack on my commutes, buying the hardcover illustrated edition of the script, signing up for the ticket lottery every day, reciting the lyrics backwards.

There are several ironies to the lyrics that rang through my head. I was in the world's greatest city because the lyrics said so. The underlying assumption being the city was theirs (and mine) to assign emotion or nostalgia to. When I say "theirs," I mean both the resurrected colonizers and the colonial subjects speaking as them. The danger being this precise juxtaposition of america's creation and its reclamation by colonial subjects.

What was even scarier was that I believed it. Because I trusted not just the writers & performers but the histories that brought them to this land, *Hamilton* was, perhaps, the greatest betrayal of imagination.

By construction, the ekphrasis that is *Hamilton* relies on both the colonial and colonized imagination—both the humanization of the colonial myth and the desire for colonial subjects to be represented within the colonial project despite erasure. The lyrics do not acknowledge the colonial legacy of america; they become it.

Had there been a *Hamilton* for Palestine—and I don't think there ever could be, due to the history of colonization and enslavement unique to america's creation—would I be anything less than distraught with rage? Imagine it: Palestinian actors dressing up as their European colonizers, telling a naturally humanized rendition of the creation of israel, which happened at their own expense. What makes this idea so inconceivable to me?

If I said my understanding of american nationalistic art began and ended with my childhood, I'd be lying. I had a firsthand understanding of the settler colonial machine. I understood the violences that created america and how my family fit into these violences. This, too, was the colonial imagination manifesting itself: I was investing myself in finding a home within the colonial project insofar as I was becoming entrenched in it. What is the expense of such a visibility *within* the colonial imagination? How are we to exist, if at all possible, in the focal point of these systems without being consumed by them?

*

Summer 2018: israel committed a several-month-long campaign slaughtering Palestinian protestors in Gaza, again. I was one of several hundred protestors, crowded inside a church in Boston on Nakba Day. The sky was gray with grief and downpour . . . I wanted to feel hopeful about the large turnout of non-Palestinian allies. I also felt a need to be around only Palestinians in this time of mourning.

A man from Gaza read the names of all the martyred protestors. Others spoke too; one speaker, a Black professor, looked around the room, and said, "So raise your hand if you, in your heart of hearts, believe that we can free Palestine."

I admit that I did not raise my hand. I admit that I flashed back to every aforementioned moment, therein reminded of how deeply entrenched I was in the colonial machine. Few raised their hands. Or perhaps I'm misremembering the proportion—funny how grief works like that.

The professor continued, telling us our thinking was completely ahistorical. Even in circumstances arguably more hopeless than Palestine, organized people always triumph over systems of oppression. Always. So why not believe in Palestine's liberation? Why not actually believe that the liberation of Palestine is not only plausible but inevitable?

The room was silent.

No one had ever asked me this question, especially in as hopeless of a moment as that day. But maybe that was exactly why I needed to hear it—among the several first steps toward the physical liberation of Palestine is imagining it. In many ways, this imagination starts with art, and yet, as a writer myself, I have little interest in writing Palestine in a way that is digestible to the colonial imagination, or in justifying our humanity to a system—meaning both the state *and* the people who build it—that finds our existence inconvenient at best. Because if not, then what is the distinction between the consumption of my art and every other ekphrasis on a fragmented nationalism set to unmake us?

*

*In which the (Arab) author imagines stolen israeli art:*

| THIS IS NOT A WALL | THIS IS NOT A WALL | THIS IS NOT A WALL |
| THIS IS NOT A WALL | THIS IS NOT A WALL | THIS IS NOT A WALL |
| THIS IS NOT A WALL | THIS IS NOT A WALL | THIS IS NOT A WALL |
| THIS IS NOT A WALL | THIS IS NOT A WALL | THIS IS NOT A WALL |
| THIS IS NOT A WALL | THIS IS NOT A WALL | THIS IS NOT A WALL |
| THIS IS NOT A WALL | THIS IS NOT A WALL | THIS IS NOT A WALL |
| THIS IS NOT A WALL | THIS IS NOT A WALL | THIS IS NOT A WALL |
| THIS IS NOT A WALL | THIS IS NOT A WALL | THIS IS NOT A WALL |
| THIS IS NOT A WALL | THIS IS NOT A WALL | THIS IS NOT A WALL |
| THIS IS NOT A WALL | THIS IS NOT A WALL | THIS IS NOT A WALL |
| THIS IS NOT A WALL | THIS IS NOT A WALL | THIS IS NOT A WALL |
| THIS IS NOT A WALL | THIS IS NOT A WALL | THIS IS NOT A WALL |
| THIS IS NOT A WALL | THIS IS NOT A WALL | THIS IS NOT A WALL |

*

I will return, dear reader, to a moment in my aforementioned trip to Palestine. As you may recall, we ended our trip in Jaffa: a city on the Mediterranean that was the landmark of much of my grandfather's nostalgia. I was walking the city with a Jewish friend of mine. They were my shoulder after visiting ethnically-cleansed villages and the segregated city of Jerusalem where my grandparents once resided. I was theirs after encountering our first instance of anti-Semitism at an israeli settlement, after going through the Holocaust Museum, and after hearing all the ways their ancestral trauma was exploited by the zionist state.

I say this not to equate our experiences—that is a key component of israel's colonial imagination. The common thread in our experiences, however, is this distortion and unwriting of history, committed by the colonial imagination—the realization that despite our memory and the representations we were fed, israel has failed all of us.

After walking through the marbled, opulent streets, after touching the Mediterranean Sea for the first time, after photographing the architecture, I believe it was my friend who said first: "This is fake. It's all fake."

And it was. Even though we were in it, physically touching and breathing it, the city we were experiencing was the physical manifestation of the colonial imagination. I'm saying the blood was not only on our hands; the blood was in our minds. We were staring right into the heart of the beast.

The colonial imagination isn't just the checkpoints, walls, eradicated villages, and families with concrete barriers through their houses; it is also opulence built over that wreckage. It is residents who are convinced they live in the greatest city in the world.

It was here, at this moment, I first realized my memory of Palestine was a misappropriation of my displaced family's experience, and no matter how much (un)learning I did, nothing would restore that original memory. Nothing would reconcile my Palestine with my family's memory of.

The liberated Palestine will not look like the Palestine that existed before it needed liberation; we must imagine it outside of its colonial reality. The land has gone from country to no man's land to country once more. The streets, heavy with language both new and familiar; the hillsides, repaved, empty of gazelles; the villages, unimaginable in the overgrowth. Would you believe that after all of this, I can see the land only through its postcolonial symbols?

I don't know how else to say this: there is always a hillside. There is always an animal, wandering or flying, and how easily a gazelle becomes a flock of eagles.

And above all, there is always an ocean, a border, a wound festering from earth to blood-fed earth, from sea to shining sea.

# The Ghosts of the Exhibit Reveal Themselves (Triptych)

## I. *into the lines of kuffiyat we stitch our generations*

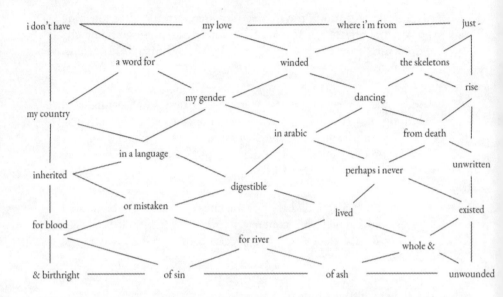

## II. *into the lines of kuffiyat we stitch our generations (post-bullet holes)*

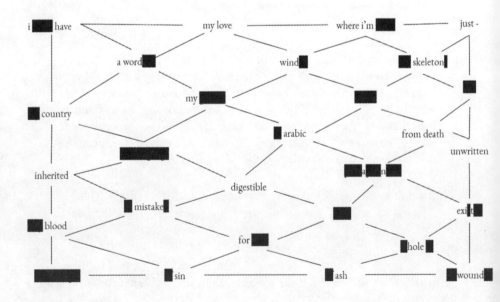

FIRE FIRE FIRE EVERYWHERE FIRE FIRE FIRE EVERYWHERE
THIS IS NOT A GAZE ELLE GAZE
& PEACE & PEACE & PEACE & PEACE & PEACE &
(quiet) PEACE & PEACE

This is
Object permanence — What did I know of — Hunger — Which moved
I have mustered — Enough tears — While you sleep — My father's ocean — Rising inch by inch — "RE FIRE
Confessing — The number of days — To drown — The shore — Of tel aviv
I parted — I have wanted — Love — More than history
With my mother — At the country — Of skin — In the dream
You are — young — Again — It is spring — In the greening valley
I swear — God — Loves us — I swear — God loves us
Will — Open — Our tombs — To windows — For the sea
Soaring — Like history — Above — The open — Page
I danced along — The spine of — The shore — Built myself — In the sand
No I — Built myself — I become — Anoth
I don't walk — I fly — In ascension — 's presence — Transfiguring

FIRE FIRE EVERYWHERE FIRE FIRE FIRE EVERYWHERE
THIS IS NOT A GAZE THIS IS NOT A GAZ INTO ME

95

# The Ghosts of the Exhibit Are Screaming (Palinode)
*after Jan-Henry Gray*

The Arab American Institute DMed me on Twitter to say my work reminds them of Kamal Boullata's. I thanked them. But, in truth, I have never read Boullata's work. I have never pored over Kanafani. Though I won an award named after him. I have never finished Said's *Orientalism*. I have never studied Darwish as well as. I won't finish that sentence. He is the only poet my family can quote from memory. The first time Teita read my work, she opened to a poem titled *Guacamole*, said she likes avocados. Aunt Tammy asked why my first chapbook didn't contain a poem about her. I wonder if she Read it. Every time I mention a book, my father jokes about not knowing *how to* read. He graduated with a degree he did not want. The degree he wanted would have required more Reading. A former white friend said some of my family members speak like they're *illiterate*. It wasn't until her funeral that I discovered my great aunt spent her early life teaching English to fellow Palestinians fleeing to america. She died before I could show her any of my poems. Her brother, Nabil, is always the first to like my poems on Facebook. He says he wrote poetry in Arabic back in Ramallah. He says poetry should terrify politicians, especially the american ones. He is the only blood relative I write for. I don't expect white people to understand how to Read this. I want them only to understand who I wish harm in the reading of me. Most of my family will die before reading this, and I think I'm okay with that. Not a year goes by without someone saying my poetry reminds them of Remi Kanazi's. I wonder if they've read anyone besides him. Naomi Shihab Nye was the only Palestinian ever assigned to me in a classroom. She was my first lesson in gratitude. The first time I met Fady Joudah, I realized I needed to spend more time Reading all of us. The first time I Read Hala Alyan's *Atrium*, I cried in the shower for 30 minutes. The first time I met Randa Jarrar, she yelled at a white imperialist on stage at a poetry festival. It was then I mourned the upbringing I could have had with an auntie like her around. When my mother read *Him, Me, Muhammad Ali*, she said reading a book has never made her feel this way. My mother will never Read my poems, and I know I'm okay with that. My brother is the only blood family I trust with all of my poems, and I think I like it that way. I've spent too much time wondering if I was the *first queer Palestinian to*—I couldn't understand the violence of completing that sentence. There are a thousand Palestinians buried beneath this poem, and none of them are speaking. Someone who turned out to be my cousin DMed me on Instagram, identifying herself as queer. She said she Sees me. To think, I was taught to consider myself alone in this. I didn't know *how to* Read then. I still don't, I think. Sometimes I carry a Palestinian's book around with me, even if I have no intention of reading or Reading it. This is how we Cousin each other. This is how we Return to each other anyways. I think we are always Returning.

## the ghosts of the dead sea rewrite the history of drowning

*after Patrick Kindig*

sink [ the bodies ] sink [ unholy ] sink [ in their own ] sink sink [
home ] sink [ the bodies ] sink [ i lift ] sink [ zion's expense ] sink [ in
skin ] sink [ & bone ] sink sink [ coarse & crystalline ] sink [ & wound
] sink [ i swallow ] sink [ or inhabit ] sink [ hot earth ] sink [ welling ]
sink [ into me ] sink sink [ converging ] sink [ topography ] sink [ of
shattered ] sink [ silt ] sink [ i betrayed ] sink [ my ] sink sink [ self ]
sink [ country ] sink [ not ] sink sink [ my ] sink [ or maybe ] sink [
i'm written ] sink [ into betrayal ] sink [ or death ] sink [ a calm ] sink
sin[ earth salt ]k sink [ holy salinity ] sink sink [ of avulsion ] sink sink
[ holy ] sink [ escape ] sink [ of fluid ] sink [ entombed ] sin [ in its
own] sin [ ghost ] sin [ town ] sin [ say Khalil ] sink [ i'm sorry ] sin [
say Gaza ] sink [ i failed ] sin [ say ocean ] sin [ i could not ] sin [
swallow ] sin [ your mirror ] sin [ horizon ] sin [ i am ] sin sin [
everything ] sin [ you are ] sin [ not ] sin [ the history ] sin sin sin [
perhaps ] sin [ is in ] sin [ the blood ] sin sin [ you name ] sin [ parallel
] sin sin [ or maybe ] sin [ the name ] sin [ is a story ] sin sin [ written
in ] sin [ blood ] sin sin [ in flesh ] sin [ which is ] sin [ its own ] sin [
holy ] sin [ sound ] sin [ reverberating ] sin sin [ thick ] sin [ in its own
] sin [ scatter ] sin [ diffusion ] sin [ say we ] sin [ were never ] sin [
light ] sin [ worthy ] sing [ praise ] sing [ your birthright ] sing [ sunset
] sing sing [ pas- ]sing [ reflection ] sing [ unto ] sing [ not my ] sing [
entirety ] sing [ praise ] sing [ the boy ] sing [ who wandered ] sing [
into me ] sing [ searching ] sing sing [ for air ] sing [ to build ] sing [
God ] sing [ from lifeless ] sing [         ] sing sing [ holy ] sing [ the
dead ] sing [ who walk ] sing [ in me ] sing [ & become ] sing [ story
] sing [ strange fiction ] sing [ biblical ] sing [ save for ] sin [ salvation
] sing [ rise ] sing [ risen ] sing [ rise ] sing [ rise ] sing sing [ rise ] sing
[ martyr ] sing [ unearth ] sing sing [ human stay ] sing [ human ] sing
[ free ] sing [ fly ] sing [ fly ] sing [ levitate ] sing sing [ fly ] sing [ fly
] sing [ by means ] sing sing [ of ghost- ] sing [ fluid ] sing [ refu- ]sing
sing [ its own ] sing [ weight ] sing sing sing

## ars poetica in which every pronoun is a Free Palestine

& so it is written: the settlers will steal God's land & FREE PALESTINE
will curse the settlers with an inability to season FREE PALESTINE's food,

a sunburn the shape of the settler dictator's face on everyone who will claim
FREE PALESTINE's earth but not FREE PALESTINE's skin

soil-stained. there. FREE PALESTINE said it. no one really owns anything FREE
PALESTINE didn't unwrite to make it so—FREE PALESTINE's sea

*israeli*; FREE PALESTINE's sky *israeli* but not FREE PALESTINE's thunder—
the blame will always be FREE PALESTINE's & so this will be called an accurate

history; the expense of FREE PALESTINE's visibility, willed in bloodied cloth—
or paper—FREE PALESTINE's longest suicide: FREE PALESTINE will die

in jail & become *israeli*—FREE PALESTINE will die in protest & become
kite on fire—FREE PALESTINE will call Hamas fable of every

*HEADLINE: israeli* falafel so dry FREE PALESTINE could start an intifada with it
*HEADLINE: israeli* falafel so dry FREE PALESTINE could free Palestine with it

no, FREE PALESTINE will never give FREE PALESTINE's self a name
not rooted in upheaval—FREE PALESTINE, hyphenated by settler flag:

FREE PALESTINE hyphenated by settler pronouns: FREE PALESTINE will not
pledge allegiance to Arabic. or english. FREE PALESTINE will exist

in no language; FREE PALESTINE will write poems of olive tree & checkpoint
with no free Palestine to be found; FREE PALESTINE will name the violence

& never the resurrection, like FREE PALESTINE hasn't survived impossible
histories to get here. It is written: the blood will be on FREE PALESTINE's

hands—might as well paint FREE PALESTINE's nails while FREE PALESTINE's
at it—what? is this not what FREE PALESTINE expected? did FREE

PALESTINE not think FREE PALESTINE would have the last laugh all along?

# Against Consolidation

> "There is no loneliness when you have the whole world inside of you.
> —Vanessa Meng

i want to write about the blueberries i picked from the throat of a new england fall afternoon; how my hands plucked each branch like a familiar melody.

& suddenly, it is 2008. i am small and unremarkable, standing in a blueberry orchard in northern california with my cousins. maybe summer is a form of muscle memory.

i want to write a poem about muscle memory—a phenomenon which, after decades of studies, still has no complete explanation. one theory suggests these memories undergo consolidation: the process of stabilization from short to long-term memory.

perhaps we can infer the existence of a thing without knowing its internal structure; perhaps our bodies remember a music by the hollow dancing it leaves behind—

many mathematical proofs of existence cannot explicitly construct their objects of interest. one tool for such proofs is the axiom of choice—metaphorically speaking, it too is a form of unconscious memory. it states that, given a tree with an unimaginable number of branches, it is still possible to pluck one blueberry from each branch—

that's not the point. i'm saying, choice is not inherent to every system of logic. the first time i learned this was not in the context of mathematics. or countries,      or bodies.

i want to write about my country & mean *country*. such a silly tithe, forgiving sacrifice—i want to write a poem about home & not have to mean *country*. or *death*—or how easily the two can be mistaken for one another; one could say this is a consequence of neither concept being well-defined—

logical assumptions like the axiom of choice can lead to *pathological* behaviors that violate our conceptions of mass, space, and time: for instance, it is possible to decompose one sphere into two identical spheres, hence four, hence infinitely many; from one life, springs two, hence four, hence infinitely many. one could say death is poorly defined in such a logical framework.

or perhaps every death is an unobservable construction; consider, for instance, the ancestors resurrected in every poem. how i was fluent in the language of their death before ever being fluent in the Arabic they spoke before me—*allah yerhama, allah yerhama*—

& is this not the job of the poet, much like the mathematician? to give language to that which cannot be constructed? to un-eviscerate the flesh, give muscle memory to every chaos of limbs.

1998: my earliest memory is being lost in a sea of cousins at a Christmas party. i do not stand out from the crowd until the dabke starts—the music shaking the floor beneath my feet & i dance like there is no earthquake beneath me; i dance & part my cousins like every ocean split before me; like my body knew i was Palestinian before i did—

or maybe it was the lurch of my gut the last time i visited my queer aunt's unmarked grave; how even in remembrance, her ghost was but an erasure of her former self.

it is important to mention, the last person i loved was buried in the same cemetery, just yards away, & yet, i have spanned entire galaxies & failed poems trying to reconstruct her laughter; how we remember not the beloved but the music they left behind—how, the last time i visited her grave, the gray skies parted, no metaphor, leaking light for the first time all week & in coincidence or faith, i am inclined to call that grace–

i want to write about tiny miracles: i woke up this morning. i woke up this morning. one could call this an instance of *pathological* behavior.

or maybe the first pathological behavior was when i mentioned the word *country*. or the space between countries & bodies in line 6. perhaps, since this is a poem about memory, it is discontinuous by necessity; there are hands, hence there will always be breakage—

neurological theory argues against some forms of consolidation; says, some memories never stabilize, but are encoded in parallel architectures. this suggests we encode reality in multiplicities, hence, every perception of reality is, by construction, a multiverse of complexity.

i want to write about the first Palestinian i met in grad school like she wasn't a miracle; or maybe every Palestinian is a parallel universe.

i want to write about new year's eve in Bethlehem: the house, swelling with cousins & pillowfight laughter. i want to talk about george, who was always first to throw the pillow but had the sweetest face when his mother came around; his father outside, roasting kabab, talking about those fuckers & checkpoints ruining his morning commute; & nathalie who paraded her hand-stitched thobes throughout the house like she owned the place & in the same breath, told us how jesus cured her cancer before the chemo could; i want to write about nadia who knew more english than her mother but counted down to midnight in arabic; the whole house, dancing to a music they didn't know but understood; i want to remember my homeland this way: the city alight but not ablaze.

i want to write about nights in Palestine where the last thing we thought about was death; about being smoked out in Ramallah like she knows she'll rise with barbed wire teeth & a steel-tipped boot to the face; that reality exists without saying, so give us tonight to dance without words—

let me remember, first, the dance & not the ensuing exile; let me write about home
without writing its unbecoming—

i confess, i've spent too much time revolving around my own unbecoming; the way time
dilates around a black hole, reality diverging at the point where not even light escapes—

i confess, dear reader, that by reading this you have become my new test subject: i speak
not of this poem, but of the memory of it—the parallel worlds your mind will inhabit,
patching together my every image in your universe of perception.

i mean: there will always be a universe in your mind, & in that universe there will always
be a Palestine with children laughing.

men have turned entire countries into test subjects without their consent. neither the
men nor countries are named so as to restrict them from the universes of this poem.

& it follows that every poem is a false god; maybe not in sin but in the confession of it:
in the unraveling between poem          & reality          & perception of poem:
i began this poem          THE SYSTEM DOES NOT CONVERGE          with blueberries
with muscle memory          THE SYSTEM DOES NOT CONVERGE          & hands—
          (or maybe i never had control over the narrative—)
being ill-defined          THE SYSTEM DOES NOT CONVERGE
when i say          THE SYSTEM DOES NOT CONVERGE          his hands smelled
          THE SYSTEM DOES NOT CONVERGE          like blueberries,
california, 2008:          THE SYSTEM DOES NOT CONVERGE
i am small & insignificant          THE SYSTEM          philadelphia, 2015:
          (yes, he made a massacre of me—
          (yes, i was his     for the taking—
          DOES NOT          i am small
          CONVERGE          i am insignificant
the poem is  circling back          THE SYSTEM DOES NOT          & diverging
the poem assumes multiple          CONVERGE          realities,
meanings          THE SYSTEM DOES NOT CONVERGE          the hands
in this way          THE SYSTEM FAILS          the poem intersects with
          TO CONVERGE          the reality of the reader
the poem remembers          THE SYSTEM DOES NOT          what the reader cannot
the hands,          CONVERGE
          THE SYSTEM DOES NOT CONVERGE          always—
          (the hands,  the poem remembers always          the hands—
          THE SYSTEM DOES NOT CONVERGE
          THE POEM DOES NOT CONVERGE
          THE POEM FAILS TO CONVERGE

# ars poetica with parallel dimensions

> i must confess, this softness is often an endless
well
> i fall into, the way a snake chases itself into
itself. on tamer days
> i blame the fruit for their thick
ripening & not the small jealousies
> endangering the honeybee;
some days i cannot distinguish desire
> from extinction—
every love of mine demands blood
> -shed, of a hunter
's lineage; o exile my exile, that i could write
> our laced talons
into metal wings; that we could
> un-cauterize the crimson sky
& fly into a sunset
> spilling blood that is not our own—that i
could turn two mirrors in on themselves, unraveling
those infinite & countable dimensions:

somewhere, i pluck an apple     & a parallel self suffers
the expulsion, itself     ancestry rippling across space, itself
timeless; in this reality, i lose     a country
for another eden     to blossom beneath
a more forgiving stratosphere;
i confess, i am more vengeful than my oppressors
deem me; my disposition, a learned
burial—i fang so hard
it louds my smile, writes my cyanide ducts
into gentle rain;
in truth, i wish my oppressors an eternity
of carnage
for every country stolen
from us, from all of my loved ones,
the way infinity plus infinity is just
infinity; forever fails us
like that; our eternity is the moment
between child's fist
& soldier's gun & therefore, is everything
but child's fist
& soldier's gun ; i know threat
is not object but state

of being; i love him, so he's everyone's

                                    threat; i bloody

my hands for him, so he must be god

                      of somewhere; i know heaven

is a poem i can survive the end of; i know holy

                                  is waking up

with a knotted neck on a red sofa in philadelphia

                                      crowded

with all of my loved ones; i know that

                          is, itself, a country

even i can have

                  faith in—

## Before Apocalypse

or, *an ode to fighting over the check with my frickin Ayrabs*

And blessed are the Bamboozled, for they have inherited
brief nourishment, yes, at my expense. Come side-eye, hand
slap, the *Allah* of teita's prayers, even though she too
is a *LeaveATwentyInYourCarSoYouHaveToAcceptIt* type—

because what parts of us weren't inherited from a light
of understandable distance—the argheela's smoke unravelling
in violet dusk, trailing to a landscape not smoldering; how else
to say *alive* but to inhale ash into our lungs; nights that leave us
fang-bare & golden may mistake this laughter for anger—I get it,

we aren't digestible alive outside of metaphor—once I wrote
a self-portrait as a snake & it was a happy poem, despite
the politician who damned us to that venom—in truth,
this was my brother's face after I beat him

to the waiter & paid for both of our dinners. Yes, that was me,
frowning & shaking my head after Summer beat me once
because she was closer to the chip reader & Noor, who leaned
his whole body out of the car to slap Hazem's credit card

away from the parking paystation. We've been here
before—offering the brief inconvenience of ourselves
because we don't know when, let alone if, there will be
a next time, & we know apocalypse. Well. We know the sound
of the belching sun as it swallows us whole. Noor says God

is written into every corner of the Arabic language, however
subconscious, so it must follow that every time two or more of us
are gathered, it is an act of divinity—we cannot give each other
a tomorrow, the sun will never betray us, & so we make it
inescapable as the *no* unspoken in our mother's every *inshallah*—
say, this is how we pray      without ever making a sound.

# Ode to Mennel Ibtissam singing *Hallelujah* on The Voice (France), translated in Arabic

*with thanks to Marwa Helal*

اهي ليبت بصرخة .. تسمعي ليلا وليس بشخص ما قد رای الفرح

maybe if , ash & smolder way the – tongue own my in never but song this heard i've

there's – it birthed who fire the not & gospel become can , mouth right the in seen

a , arabic your of fall minor the – flame still is , core its at which , prayer bluest your

god finds , tremor oud shrieks country a , somewhere – before us failed has which flag

above throne his builds man a , somewhere – fifth the , fourth the – lungs tenor on

all , earth still – lullaby into them writes & song ceaseless their claims , undoing the

i've ,yes – tongues moonlit in , brash , spoke who children of empty , streets marble

ever you – handed- bloody , doves the twinned – history this from devil the archangel-ed

learned we land the somewhere – song its in voice your lose you'd much so country a love

from skyward & permanent , contour memorized every – inherited we land the also is

was always history our , sing you because – another unmothering metal the to up back hurling not-bombs

how – you in translation refused revolution the : unwinged paradise without country a

to sent & bleached i arabic an , this – hollow & fullthroated us – march victory

shoots english – days these alive me keep can words demand ,& ي its

somebody's like , confident speak to me demands & teeth few so because , colonizer a

who arabic your , first , was it – throat my in itself of home a my down arrows cold

– outdrew prayer from ,to singing worth god a made – key major a in make didn't fist broken[1]

– throat your in organ the Hallelujah'ed

– resurrect lungs your Palestine the , Hallelujah

– you through running dead restless of choir the , Hallelujah

– stone & wind its , earth this of you , Hallelujah

– you of sound the at trembling breathing everything

* Rules of engagement: if the poem is to be read from right to left, it is to be observed unredacted. If the poem is to be read from left to right, the reader must impose redactions of the English language. If the poem is to be read down its right and/or left margins, it is to be sung in Mennel's voice.

# Alternate Mythologies of Exile

"Truth eats lies just as the crocodile eats the moon, and yet my witness is
the same today as it will be tomorrow."
—Marlon James

I. Mythos of Floodwater, Ending in the Promise of Return
*A Palinode*

> Say instead, the dove returned from the floodwater, bold
> -taloned, with a bloodied olive branch, feathers dirtied
>     white. The opposite of a murder is a flock
>
> of doves. The opposite of a flock of doves is a genocide. Not all
> murders are genocides, but both demand flight. We looked to wings
>     so white, we forgot they raised predatory beings,
>
> & what else could we do but emerge with new lexicon, a truer thing
> to call air: we built our Gods from the floodwater & that's
>     the story of breath. We were promised
>
> an ocean, but all we wanted was a river's saltless motion.
> Hear me: I am writing from a land where survival is no longer
>     viable. For this, I've tried to apologize, then strike
>
> match to bare earth, but both times I was the one in flames.
> I looked into the fire & found, not the absence of God,
>     but the opposite of God. & sure, past tense
>
> implies survival, but before the fire failed at its myth-making,
> before a tower rose out from our mistranslations of wind, before
>     we filled our boat with a tragic notion of symmetry
>
> to survive those floodwaters, before we told ourselves there was
> an Eden to mourn the loss of, we were never skyward beings.
>     This is what it means for our whole existence to be
>
> an apology. This being the sound our world makes as it rejects
> us. This being the sound we make, floating skyward blue: *we did this*
>     *ourselves. We did this to ourselves.*

**

I once found my second self at a mountaintop. He wore
my skin, and yes, that was my voice in his throat. We stood
                among each other in perfect trinity: two boys

& the ghosts between us. He looked to the sky & said, *Lord,*
*if this, my land, is not enough, take me as your own.*
                He drew the knife skyward. Blood pooled

in his open palm & it was not my own. I looked to the sky & said
nothing—I have lived a thousand lives without land, but none without
                a body. It wasn't that God didn't respond, but that

He responded with silence. The man who was & wasn't me lunged
towards me, knife outstretched, & perhaps I side-stepped & let his body,
                which was & was not my body, fly off of the hillside, or

perhaps, as my own knife glided itself through his neck, we locked eyes
& I saw my own face for the first time, or perhaps I let him plunge into
                me & yes, gifted him myself & became a contradiction

of. I can't tell you how this ends, but I will say the air
was calm & that meant God was with us. East of here,
                a golden field is rising. Singing. Heavy with my name.

II. Mythos of Birthright, Ending in a Return to Olympus
*A Palinode*

> "Maybe then, a return, maybe wingspan, elsewhere. I am not a proud
> beast."
> —Zaina Alsous

I was born a reckoning of
    the historic. Post -human, pre

-image. Imagine me
    this way: before a jealous god

siphoned me into mortal, I caught light
    in my bare hands & became it—

tell me Elysium is a hilltop to be
    inherited, & I'll say my father crafted me

from liquid thunder, so nothing
    could strip away that God

in me—yes, I once considered Return
    unfathomable, & yes, though it came

at the expense of bodies including
    my own, I Returned anyways; once, a half-

soldier made a labyrinth of my country & I did not
    choke him with golden twine

but with heel pressed to throat because
    it was the softest part of me; once,

I was beheaded, & 3 heads grew back
    in its place; a slice & another

one & another one watched me transcend
    my oppressor's recursion—once,

the sun tried to swallow me
    whole, & I grew wings to say, *see me*

*eye-to-eye*—once, I was unwinged
        but came back re-bodied

in a flurry of blossoms—it is prophecy:
        you cannot kill us when we exist

this loudly; what you call *water*, I call
        *ancestor*—drown me in that river,

I'll emerge with golden skin—
        suffocate me in my dead, I'll be anything

but sin; & when I Returned
        in spite of everyone

fallen before me—split heel, head
        of snakes un-tethered—my people

looked upon me, open-armed,
        like I was nothing

less than a God, knowing
        it was the prettiest lie: I am,

therefore I parallel—I am,
        therefore, a multitude—so let me

be brief: let me be
        light—what you call *raising*

*hell*, I call *reclamation*
        *song*—listen: I have lived so many

lives in this body, & there is no greater gift
        than the sound

your stolen land makes
        as you ascend back

through its fields, press your palm
        to its earth, in fracture,

& crown yourself
        in its name.

III. Mythos of Paradise, Without Ending
*A Palinode*

> "whatever returns from oblivion returns to find a voice:"
>
> \- Louise Glück

Consider Elysium. Once more, as only you could
        inherit it. Let's say your heaven is the point
on the compass where East & West fold into each other
        like a prayer – by arriving here you forgot there was any
direction to mourning; you tried to imagine the absence of border
        as all the ghosts you failed to contain, but have yet to imagine
its opposite: arcadia sprawling without notion of line
        or limit. You've gotten yourself to a mountaintop,
but all you want to do is apologize for it; every notion of sky
        being contingent upon the promise of soil & rain –
let's start there: at the boundary between life
        & slumber. Let's say someone greets you
on the other side, says *don't worry, there is nothing left*
        *to grieve.* You begin to follow them upwards into
the underbrush, not noticing the path before you. This
        is your ecosystem of thought. Here, azaleas mid-
plume – six-legged mouth, tongue of lipstick fire. Flight
        means it's springtime. There isn't a heat
-loss to mourn. Here, eyelashes erupting from a small sun –
        this and every other shelter for tiny wanderers who pluck
highbush berries from branches the weight of air.
        You arrive at a clearing. Surrounding the clearing
is a forest. At the edge of the forest is the same someone
        who greeted you upon arrival. Let's call them
Forgiveness. Let's say Forgiveness is a God
        with so many faces, they have no face at all: here,
your mother's face fading into the bark of a willow tree;
        behind her, your father laced in moss; beneath him,
an ancestry you have yet to imagine. You walk into the forest,
        seeking its center, only to arrive back where you began.
Let's say a century has passed, and Forgiveness' faces
        expanded, factorial. Forgiveness laughs, says, *it is impossible*
*to know how the earth bends beneath you – from what shape*

*your land inherits its emptiness* – so you try again, re-enter that
same, face-studded wood: here, azaleas wailing; here, a funeral
quiet, blossomed: though the dead have names written
in song, you have yet to find your own. This is your heaven,
& you've decided you deserve the lilted rush of a dragonfly's
wings double-visioned, a croak echoing unpoisoned, but have yet
to imagine a mirror – a water's surface – so you strike match.
Set fire, and arrive at Forgiveness once more. They laugh,
saying, *it's not radical to set fire to a land if it was never yours
to mourn*, so you start again. Set fire, recursion. Forgiveness
says, *you look into that & see only destruction. What is a fire
but the light's refusal to die – look unto what is left behind. Look
at how the light touches it. Becomes it. That means it was once
home to something.* You speak back, for the first time:
*I'm not asking to be made an angel of, I'm just saying I need my wings
back.* You begin again, not searching for a center, & from the ash
& soot, a temple. From the temple, empire. From empire,
fire. From fire, multiverse, wingspan, soundless death. There is
a you, you cannot find, outside of you dreaming all of this.
You cannot take root. It's springtime, & what can you do but look into
eternity's face & reject it. This is your loneliest sound. You
step into the light, & Forgiveness is a daffodil in a wooded clearing.
You palm the daffodil, inhale it; allow Forgiveness to enter
& your throat ruptures. This means you've earned your blood;
you've welcomed dusk into your jaundiced heaven, now
pooling silver. You are heaven's first body of water. You know how
this needs to end: through the surface, Forgiveness takes
your image. There's a blade in your palm, & you've earned it
this time. If your first violence was existing, your second
was being worthy of a good fight. You step
onto the water's surface. Your footprints redden
the silver lake. You're running like you haven't abandoned;
the distance between you & Forgiveness, collapsing – the lake
mirroring no sky, no sky but absence of – here, a summer, endless
as myth. Here, a restless boy, his silly pleasure. Here, hands
that made you parting golden wheat – this is your country, shallow
-graved, & for this you will not apologize. Forgiveness laughs,

coughs up flags the color of blood's mythology. Forgiveness laughs
        as you twist the blade on the way out. Forgiveness spills light
& from that light liquid flames – the lake beneath you dissolving into
        molten ash. Forgiveness cackles – *is this your country? Always*
*to end ablaze?* & you do not thank Forgiveness for misinterpreting
        your history. You slice and another flag pools; Forgiveness
stops laughing. *Child – we both know neither of us even exist* – you lodge
        your fist into Forgiveness' throat. You pull out Forgiveness'
tongue, which is not your tongue, and slice it into a thousand
        pieces. You say, *all I know of your image is the right end of a sword*
*on fire. I know forgiveness, not as body, but ecosystem – this is my country,*
        *and you're not welcome here.* Forgiveness shrieks, unspeakable.
This being the sound of history written by those who took their magic
        back – this is your curse, & it is anything but
hymn: at the center of every mythos is a brutalized
        body; at the center of every brutalized body is a history
untold; at the center of the center of every mythos is a history waiting
        to rise brutally through our bodies – a fist shoots skyward
from the molten earth, and from one stems two, no – four, no –
        an infinite ancestry – undead & snarling from the quaking
ground; Forgiveness, swallowed in fist & rapture; a magmal ocean
        rising – you levitate in their arms; from the right distance
it may resemble a throne. Though you began in search for a legend of,
        you found, instead, an ars poetica written in blood. You
decide to give it a physiology, perhaps, a genome, perhaps lineage –
        there isn't a name for a countryless people, but at least there's
this song:


            Not a single word escapes the sunless burial.
            There are no trees to catch the restless wind.
            A mourningless dusk is coming.
            This being the sound of beginning:

## Despite Forgiveness,

I first found God        in my father's voice – hollering,   shaking
the house's 5 am stillness,              demanding me   to wake
a whole 1800 seconds ahead of schedule: *GEORGE!* **CLAP** *INTEH*
*YOUR SAMJAH IS COLD!* **CLAP CLAP** *UP!!* knowing damn well
the breakfast samjah isn't even cooking, but He knows I can't resist

an egg yolk, not at this hour, even if the whites are burnt on the bottom
and uncooked on top –   I'm grateful –     the yolk still leaks,
spills and glosses the porcelain in an opaque tide; my khobzeh still
catches light for me to swallow –            on mornings like these,
I give myself permission to love that swell        and burst; to love
the broken, leaky thing in all its simple     being – I first found God

in my father's brand       of imperfect: flat          -foot, tooth
        -gap, the island of skin     between a non-existent hairline
& a mis-matched toupee; I still don't know if *samjah* actually translates
to sandwich, or if it was another word of my father's invented Arabic:
lexicon of rushed adaptation; my first lesson in abandonment  being His
contradiction of tongues: my father breaking & re-inventing this

language every morning,     even when neither of us wanted to wake;
I found a holiness in that     unwanting – in the distance between
 yesterday's simmers & today's       benign startles: one night of un
-existing, so maybe it's fair to say, my father existed most loudly in that
        liminal space of half-light,        and maybe that made Him God

                          *

-like; last week, my brother moved out, called and said the first thing
he missed was our father's brief    inconveniences: a premature, waking
holler; the burn stain & smoke stutter of his frying pan; being called into
the living room at midnight just to be asked about a run-down, decades
-old thing on Facebook Marketplace He definitely isn't going to
        hide    from anyone, along with the fact that it cost $7, which is
maybe the point of it all. I too missed Him most   like this: mouth agape
mid-roar,   no context. Or maybe I left    because I needed to miss Him

like I missed Him that night ten years ago, when Mama woke me up
mid-slumber,     dropped me off at the neighbors & said, *His heart,*
*His heart, Baba's heart is failing Him     beneath surgical light* – in truth,
none of this was  unexpected:    He whose father died   of a heart

117

attack, whose father died of a broken heart, who fathered a godless    son
beneath that light; were He to die, my small brain pictured him & all
               those churchless Sundays –        all my little guilts turned
skyward;          those days,    I'd speak to God

in the same way I'd speak to my father: open-palmed, begging
for light; always a laugh        and then a whimper – heaven is
               exclusive by nature –        wouldn't exist without
smolder and bitten fruit; I've been searching for a construct of
paradise that has no borders,    no bodies    displaced thereof; a heart
is a kind of border,    so I know mine will kill me    someday: inheritance
          is inheritance is    autosomal until    dominant, until

                              *

definition – yesterday, the lab tech cut    into a brain specimen,
               prodded,    dug until the trigeminal nerve    exposed itself
like a slit gut, and there        I wondered what my body would look like
outside of itself –    would they prod my post-mortem atria with metal
               fingers, say *this      is where the flood begat    thrombosis, begat the swell
and dam break?* Would they load me onto a slide,    waning arterial, to call
microscopy; say *this calcified border was once      a runny nucleus & not stone
who cast the river      turbulent?* Not all fluid adapts    with the ease

of water – take for instance, my father      post-survival: yolk-less egg
   for sunrise, bloodless    meat for dusk; with age,    He swelled
like moonlight, and here    I remember this unlearning is not amnesia,
          but merely        hushed night    -fall: heavied eyelids:
all my life has been a series of rushed awakenings   from never knowing

I was asleep       to begin with: my father stayed,        and I became
          grateful; another sibling died, and I    wrote her into
angel; year after year    after, I let myself die every night; some days,  in
grief, others, this inheritance of breathless mourning; these days, a small
-throated dragon breathes restless air down my throat, and He keeps me

alive    for now; expands my lungs    until they swallow an atmosphere;
some days, He wakes me    unprompted; roars like only    my father
can,    God-like: the only inconvenience    vast enough to wake me;
I've slept through hurricanes but never through my father's

small heresies – these days, I wake open-irised – laugh full-throated
& darlinged – I've lost so many   years to the sleepless haze of a blood
   deplete of air: once       I lost a sibling with the roundest laugh,

& so I've forgotten the sound     the air makes as it escapes us,
          and what is laughter if not the most familiar ghost?
How do I  tell someone they have a dead girl in their throat? How do I
laugh with all my teeth when I have a dead country     for a heart?

                              *

Another cousin died of a heart attack last week. Didn't   make it
to fifty – collapsed at work    mid-day. This is how we know our country
hasn't left us but, instead, embeds itself    in our ticking   organs; every
day is a small catastrophe     when you've lived on this side of Eden;
          if it was hands       that built us, we must be     made
impermanent: every shadow       birthed of a distant and unattainable
light: that the lord would build   us in fatal symmetries only for us
     to break them –   to find God   in that breakage –   so maybe –

maybe heaven is   a runny egg yolk – maybe heaven is   a punctured
     membrane –       I slice and a country     pools onto my plate,
alit –   I scoop it into my mouth,       and it is no less inheritance
than irony –   nourishment       from lifeless soma; death
     in its most luminous       and mitochondrial intake:

I hear people are making graves embedded into the roots of trees
now – imagine:   a Palestinian dies, and an olive tree   grows back
in their place; a Palestinian dies,     and their body, seeping  chlorophyll,
   still catches   light   from a somewhere   that becomes them—

                              *

I first found myself   in a confluence     of light: when the sun broke
itself into a continuum     through a bus window –   when the glitter
of my cheek     caught my eye in a passing   reflection, I found myself:

                              There. And I was
no God but that  of tilted smile and beak-framed nose. And maybe that
was the holiest thing  about me – I found God, and He was  outside my
     self – I found     myself, and I was not     everything –

And it's at moments like these when I think of Him & wonder
if He's eaten today; somedays, He's my father, or my brother
by blood     or choice – He is always a thousand miles south
of me and when I ask,       *have you slept today?* I mean,
     *I love you –*     I mean,
                    *do you love me enough*
                              *to stay?*

                              119

# Notes

The Song of Ash sections of "Inheritance: a Translation" were written in response to the Haifa wildfires of December 2016, for which the israeli state not only insinuated that Palestinian "terrorism" was among the causes of this natural disaster, but also refused to acknowledge Palestinian aid to dousing these fires, which were destroying Palestinian land.

"Autotranslations of Surveillance" was written after, and would not exist without, Solmaz Sharif's "The Master's House."

"elegy for Home in mirrored graves" would not have happened without the poetry and friendship of Zeke Russell.

"in which you do not ask the state of israel to commit suicide" would not exist without the mentorship and Genius of Dr. Sa'ed Atshan.

Portions of the "Brief Histories of Fire" section in "Cartographies of Light" borrow language from israeli "journalist" Ben Caspit who, when writing on the imprisoning of Ahed Tamimi, said "In the case of the girls, we should exact a price at some other opportunity, in the dark, without witnesses and cameras"(Maariv online, 2017). The third section of "Cartographies of Light" borrows language from photos of the israeli apartheid wall graffiti, including personal first-hand photos. The Free (blank space) refers to the censoring of any mention of "Palestine" in graffiti in Hebron, while the state simultaneously allows "Kill the Arabs" to remain, prominently displayed.

"To All the Ghosts I've Loved Before" borrows a line from Britney Spears' "Hit Me Baby One More Time" (reading the capitalized first words of each section). The title takes its inspiration from Jenny Han's Young Adult Romance novel, *To All the Boys I've Loved Before.*

"After Balfour" is comprised of a series of cut-out erasures of the Balfour Declaration (no words were added, though words were cut out and rearranged and trimmed).

"Ekphrasis with Toothing Chainsaw in Unnamed Halhul Vineyard" was written in response to israeli settlers attacking a Palestinian vineyard with a chainsaw last year, and painting "We will reach everywhere," in the vandalism. I am curious about poetry's capacity to become a vessel for writing history, especially through the lens of diasporic distance. I wrote this poem in an invented form I call the Markov Sonnet, inspired by the probabilistic framework of the Markov chain. This model represents a sequence of actions such that one action only directly depends on the action directly preceeding it, and hence, only directly influences the next action. The Markov sonnet is to be read by considering every 3 lines in isolation, as a cause/action/effect triplet; the poem both aggressively repeats and forgets itself.

"The Ghosts of the Exhibit Reveal Themselves (Triptych)" takes its formal inspiration from Layli Long Soldier's star quilt poems (see *New Poets of Native Nations*, Graywolf 2018). The third part of this pieces is a cento, composed of lines from poems by Noor Hindi, Naomi Shihab Nye, Hala Alyan, Jessica Abughattas, Zaina Alsous, Fady Joudah, Mahmoud Darwish, Lena Khalaf Tuffaha, Deema Shehabi, Tariq Luthun, and Fargo Tbakhi.

"The Ghosts of the Exhibit are Screaming (Palinode)" is for the 2019 Wet Hot Arab Summer Cohort and the Radius of Arab American Writers.

"Before Apocalypse" is for all of my Ayrabs.

"Ode to Mennel Ibtissam" is in response to French Moroccan singer, Mennel Ibtissam, whose audition video for Voice (France)—an Arabic rendition of Hallelujah by Leonard Cohen—went viral. Afterwards, she was harassed and doxed by white supremacists due to tweets critiquing israel's bombing of Gaza as well as tweets critiquing French islamophobia, and eventually quit the competition.

"Alternate Mythologies of Exile" would not exist without the palinodes of Bradley Trumpfheller, Anne Carson, Monica Youn, and the poetry of Julian Randall and Louise Glück.

# Acknowledgments

I would like to thank the following journals and anthologies, which first published versions of poems/prose pieces in this manuscript, sometimes under different titles: *Ambit Magazine, The American Poetry Review, ANMLY (fka Drunken Boat), Apogee Journal, The Asian American Literary Review, Beloit Poetry Journal, Bettering American Poetry vol 2, Beyond Memory: an Anthology of Arab American Creative Nonfiction (University of Arkansas Press), the Blueshift Journal, Boston Review, Cordite Review, Cosmonauts Avenue, Forward—A 21st Century Flash Anthology (Aforementioned Press), F(r)iction, Hawai'i Review, Jewish Currents, jubilat, Kweli Journal, LitHub, the Margins, The Massachusetts Review, Mizna (Volume 18.2 and Volume 19.2—the Palestine Issue), Nepantla, The Paris Review, Poem-A-Day (The Academy of American Poets), PoetryNow (The Poetry Foundation), The Quarry: A Social Justice Poetry Database (Split This Rock), Rattle, The Rumpus, Scalawag Magazine, The Shallow Ends, Tinderbox Poetry Journal, Tin House,* and *Winter Tangerine.*

Some of these poems have also appeared previously in the chapbooks *al youm—for yesterday & her inherited traumas,* published by the Atlas Review in 2017, and *the specimen's apology,* published by Sibling Rivalry Press in 2019.

First and foremost, to my chosen family. To Julian—I wouldn't be a poet (let alone alive) without you; I Love you. To Jess—my moon, my luv, for your GEORGE's & other songs; I Batata you. To Hazem—for our HELLO?!'s, our O RLYs, even our GOODBYEs; you are someone I can always Return to. To Bradley—for your precision and Softness, always; my mind wouldn't be the same without you. I Poem you. To torrin—for being the first to scream with/for/among; I bb you. To Noor—for every time you pushed & inspired me to break language; I Teita you. To Xavi—nearly every memory of my most luminous days includes you; I Love you. To Marwa—I wouldn't be the poet or person I am without you; I Family you. To Jared—kharia of my heart, abu shikhakh of my life; I Brother you.

To my blood family, I know y'all are looking for your names: Tony, Susan, Tammy, & Richard. To Nabil—the first poet in my family I ever knew—and Mariette for your never-ending Love. To my grandparents, Theresa & George, Jack & Randa. To my ancestors who guide me every day. I love all of you.

I want to, from the bottom of my heart, thank everyone who read early drafts of this book (or poems therein) and helped guide and shape its journey, most especially: Julian Randall, Hazem Fahmy, torrin greathouse, James Merenda, Marwa Helal, Philip Metres, Fady Joudah, Itiola Jones, Bradley Trumpfheller, and Hanif Abdurraqib.

To RAWI (especially Wet Hot Arab-American Summer 2019 fellows), Kundiman, The Watering Hole, and the Poetry Incubator—this book wouldn't be what it is without the communities who homed me.

I am especially grateful to those who led workshops which, either directly or indirectly, helped me write poems for this book, namely Marwa Helal, Sun Yung Shin, Monica Youn, C. Dale Young, Siaara Freeman, Sophia Holtz, Emily O'Neill, Adam Hamze, Danez Smith, Delana Dameron, Terrance Hayes, Craig Santos Perez, Jennifer Tseng, and Myung Mi Kim. Thank you to all my poetry teachers, formal and informal, but most especially Ruba Ahmed, JC Todd, Vision, Larry Knight, and Rick L'Ecuyer.

To my batatas: especially Summer, Noor, Noor, Noor, Sonia, Nader, Lana, Lena, Leila, Leila, Layla, Zaina, Zeina, Fargo, Jess, Jess, Lexi, Yasmin, Hazem, Marwa, Randa, Hala, Phil, Fady, Farid, Safia, Adam, Hayan, Kamelya, Ahimsa, Rami, Ramy, Remi, Sara, Deema, Tariq, Tarik, and so many more. I Cousin you all. To my swattie sharmoutas: Delfin, Xavi, Kaitlyn, Cesar, Aaliyah, and Barbara. I Cousin you all too. To D'mani for the tenderness & support I needed while finishing this book; I bb you. To my home friends: Arun, Mara, Leah, Maria, Rachel. To Emaleigh, always, and Robin and Neil.

To my labmates, for uplifting my art despite *issus*. To Ryan for challenging and inspiring me, always. To Tanvi (aka Crazy T) for the laughter, & for having my back. To Rishi for the wine mom-ing. To Andrew for our bus rides. To Hayoun for pushing me to be a braver person. To Laith for our time in Barcelona.

I'm grateful for the literary and communal Heroes who have shaped and guided my journey, who have uplifted me (be it physically in community and/or with their work). Gratitude: Solmaz Sharif, Tommy Pico, Cathy Linh Che, Kaveh Akbar, Hala Alyan, Randa Jarrar, Marwa Helal, Safia Elhillo, Phil Metres, Farid Matuk, Danez Smith, Chen Chen, Emily Jungmin Yoon, Hayan Charara, Fady Joudah, Sun Yung Shin, Shuchi Saraswat, and Zeina Hashem Beck. And last but not least, to Craig Santos Perez, Naomi Shihab Nye, and Sa'ed Atshan for their kind words about this collection, without whom this book wouldn't exist.

Thank you to all of my poetry slam homes—to everyone at OASIS and UMass Boston Slam, to Simone and how the Cantab has homed me, to Porsha and how House Slam has homed me. To Haven, Meaghan and Hayley who have homed me. To Meatland, RebeccaLynn, Juju, and JQ who have homed me.

Last but not least: to Button Poetry for their faith in me, especially Hanif for the editorial vision + the genuine Care you gave these poems, as well as Sam and Hitomi for the work you've done to give life to this book.

## Map of Home

This book, while physically bound as an object which can be read from front to back, is not intended to be Read in such a linear manner. I've given you this book's landscape, but no map to navigate it.

Enclosed on the following page is this collection's Map of Home, or, in other words, its "True" table of contents. The following are rules of engagement:

1. Note that not every poem in this book is defined as a point on this map. Consider which poems are present, and which are missing, in making decisions on how to traverse this landscape.
   2. There is no definitive beginning or end of this map, but, instead, every poem can be seen as an entry point into the heart of the book, which, by construction, initiates a journey.
3. Every linear path on this map represents a "lineage" of poems, and each lineage either converges to an alternate myth of exile, or cycles infinitely in its traumatic loop.
4. Every lineage can be exited at any point, but consider the consequences of leaving a lineage, and consider what that brings to the next lineage at that point of entry.
5. Consider every path to be oriented from left to right, meaning a right to left traversal would be considered a breakage of map.
6. Consider the connections between these poems as conversations, which can be seen as progression or development in a narrative sense, or can be seen as contradiction, either explicitly or implicitly.
7. Consider that the path laid out in the table of contents at the front of this book cannot be defined or traversed on this map without breaking the book's landscape.
8. Consider the distinction between reading and Reading.

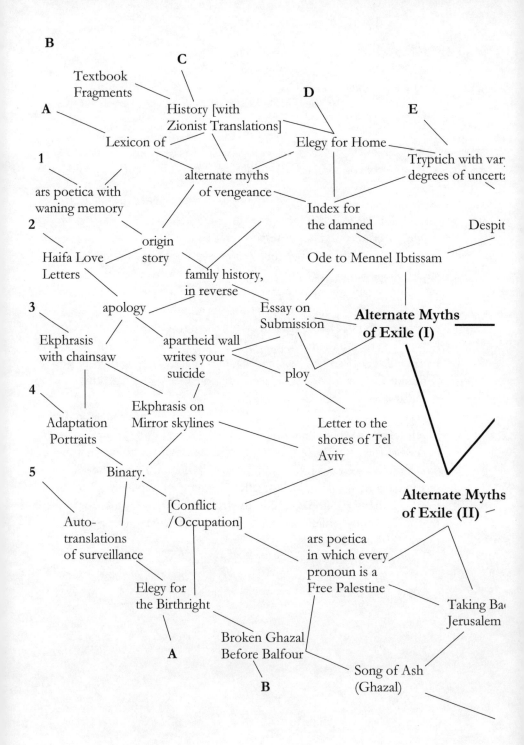

**B**

Textbook
Fragments

**C**

**A**

History [with
Zionist Translations]

**D**

Lexicon of

Elegy for Home

**E**

**1**

Tryptich with var
degrees of uncert

ars poetica with
waning memory

alternate myths
of vengeance

**2**

Index for
the damned

Despit

Haifa Love
Letters

origin
story

Ode to Mennel Ibtissam

family history,
in reverse

**3**

apology

Essay on
Submission

**Alternate Myths
of Exile (I)**

Ekphrasis
with chainsaw

apartheid wall
writes your
suicide

ploy

**4**

Adaptation
Portraits

Ekphrasis on
Mirror skylines

Letter to the
shores of Tel
Aviv

**5**

Binary.

**Alternate Myths
of Exile (II)**

Auto-
translations
of surveillance

[Conflict
/Occupation]

ars poetica
in which every
pronoun is a
Free Palestine

Elegy for
the Birthright

Taking Ba
Jerusalem

Broken Ghazal
Before Balfour

**A**

**B**

Song of Ash
(Ghazal)

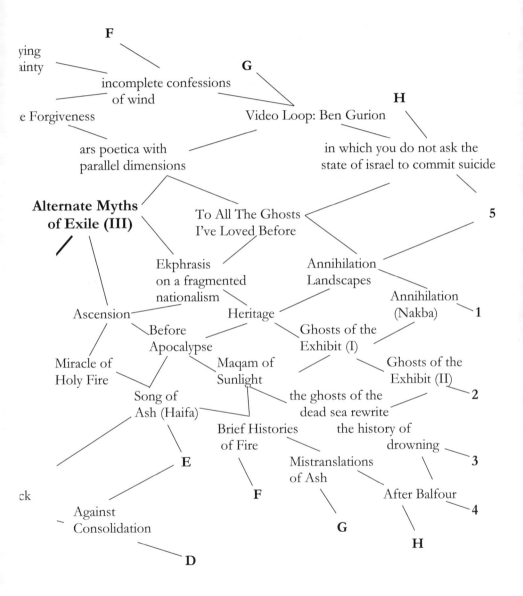

George Abraham is a Palestinian American poet from Jacksonville, Florida. They are the author of the chapbooks: *the specimen's apology* (Sibling Rivalry Press, 2019) and *al youm* (TAR, 2017). He is a board member for the Radius of Arab American Writers, as well as a Kundiman, Poetry Incubator, and Watering Hole fellow, winner of the Cosmonauts Avenue Poetry Prize, and recipient of the College Union Poetry Slam International's *Best Poet* title. Their work has been published with *the Paris Review, American Poetry Review, LitHub, Poem-A-Day,* and anthologies such as *Bettering American Poetry, Beyond Memory: an Anthology of Arab-American Creative Nonfiction,* and *Nepantla.* He is a graduate of Swarthmore College, and is currently based in Massachusetts, where he is a PhD candidate in Bioengineering at Harvard University, studying neural control of movement. *BIRTHRIGHT* is their first full-length collection of poems.

Find them on Twitter and Instagram @IntifadaBatata, or at their website: gabrahampoet.com.

# OTHER BOOKS BY BUTTON POETRY

If you enjoyed this book, please consider checking out some of our others, below. Readers like you allow us to keep broadcasting and publishing. Thank you!

Neil Hilborn, *Our Numbered Days*
Hanif Abdurraqib, *The Crown Ain't Worth Much*
Olivia Gatwood, *New American Best Friend*
Donte Collins, *Autopsy*
Melissa Lozada-Oliva, *peluda*
Sabrina Benaim, *Depression & Other Magic Tricks*
William Evans, *Still Can't Do My Daughter's Hair*
Rudy Francisco, *Helium*
Guante, *A Love Song, A Death Rattle, A Battle Cry*
Rachel Wiley, *Nothing Is Okay*
Neil Hilborn, *The Future*
Phil Kaye, *Date & Time*
Andrea Gibson, *Lord of the Butterflies*
Blythe Baird, *If My Body Could Speak*
Desireé Dallagiacomo, *SINK*
Dave Harris, *Patricide*
Michael Lee, *The Only Worlds We Know*
Raych Jackson, *Even the Saints Audition*
Brenna Twohy, *Swallowtail*
Porsha Olayiwola, *i shimmer sometimes, too*
Jared Singer, *Forgive Yourself These Tiny Acts of Self-Destruction*
Adam Falkner, *The Willies*
Kerrin McCadden, *Keep This To Yourself*

Available at buttonpoetry.com/shop and more!